BFI Film Classics

The BFI Film Classics series introduces, interprets and celebrates landmarks of world cinema. Each volume offers an argument for the film's 'classic' status, together with discussion of its production and reception history, its place within a genre or national cinema, an account of its technical and aesthetic importance, and in many cases, the author's personal response to the film.

For a full list of titles in the series, please visit
https://www.bloomsbury.com/uk/series/bfi-film-classics/

For Betz-O-Vision and the ever-resonant SLP past

Nashville

Heather Hendershot

THE BRITISH FILM INSTITUTE
Bloomsbury Publishing Plc, 50 Bedford Square, London, WC1B 3DP, UK
Bloomsbury Publishing Inc, 1385 Broadway, New York, NY 10018, USA
Bloomsbury Publishing Ireland, 29 Earlsfort Terrace, Dublin 2, D02 AY28, Ireland

BLOOMSBURY is a trademark of Bloomsbury Publishing Plc

First published in Great Britain 2025 by Bloomsbury on behalf of the
British Film Institute, 21 Stephen Street, London, W1T 1LN
www.bfi.org.uk

The BFI is a cultural charity, a National Lottery distributor, and the UK's lead organisation for film
and the moving image. We believe society needs stories. Film, television and the moving image
bring them to life, helping us to connect and understand each other better. We share the stories
of yesterday, search for the stories of today, and shape the stories of tomorrow.

Cover artwork: © Dominic Bodden
Series cover design: Louise Dugdale
Series text design: Ketchup/SE14
Images from *Nashville* (Robert Altman, 1975), © American Broadcasting Company/Paramount
Pictures Corporation; *McCabe and Mrs. Miller* (Robert Altman, 1971), © Warner Bros.; *The Last Picture
Show* (Peter Bogdanovich, 1971), © Last Picture Show Productions; *California Split* (Robert Altman,
1974), © Reno Associates; *That Cold Day in the Park* (Robert Altman, 1969), © Factor-Altman-Mirell
Films; *Thieves Like Us* (Robert Altman, 1974), © United Artists Corporation; *3 Women* (Robert
Altman, 1977), © Twentieth Century-Fox Film Corporation; *Laugh-In* (Dogby Wolfe, 1968–73),
George Schlatter–Ed Friendly Productions/Romart, Inc.; *Tanner '88* (Robert Altman, 1988), HBO
Film stills courtesy BFI National Archive

Bloomsbury Publishing Plc does not have any control over, or responsibility for, any third-party
websites referred to or in this book. All internet addresses given in this book were correct at the
time of going to press. The author and publisher regret any inconvenience caused if addresses
have changed or sites have ceased to exist, but can accept no responsibility for any such changes.

A catalogue record for this book is available from the British Library.

A catalog record for this book is available from the Library of Congress.

ISBN: PB: 978-1-8390-2894-6
          ePDF: 978-1-8390-2896-0
          ePUB: 978-1-8390-2895-3

Printed and bound in India

For product safety related questions contact productsafety@bloomsbury.com.

To find out more about our authors and books visit www.bloomsbury.com
and sign up for our newsletters.

Contents

1 A Cinema of Losers

Geoff Andrew describes *Nashville* as an 'intimate epic'.[1] That's
exactly right. And it is precisely that oxymoronic quality that makes
it so challenging to write about the film. Robert Altman's 1975 movie
is a sprawling endeavour full of big, panoramic moments, and also
a tight picture about small moments of intimacy and alienation.
It's a loud film of music and overlapping dialogue, and a quiet
film of uncomfortable silences and strange monologues. It's about
individuals concerned with themselves, in isolation or in awkward
interaction with others, but also more broadly it's about America, a
country that has reached the point of political exhaustion in the wake
of Vietnam, Nixon, assassinations – a hangover from the 1960s that
has segued into the despair and cynicism of the 1970s.

The film is extraordinarily 'easy', as Keith Carradine's character
Tom sings, meaning not 'simple', but the other sense of the word,
promiscuous, willing to do anything, willing to wander from
character to character (twenty-four of them in all), unwilling to be
tied down by any of the niceties one expects from Hollywood films,
such as a commitment to a single genre or a focus on the development
of just one or two individuals. *Nashville* is about failed attempts
at human connection, all within the context of a wider, American
moment of failure. In spite of those failures, and Altman's trademark
cynicism, the film ultimately offers fleeting moments of connection
and of guarded hopefulness.

Those moments of human connection feel timeless, and yet, if
you had to pick one film to represent 1975 America, you could not do
better than *Nashville*. One snapshot from the set helps illustrate that
bigger picture. Nixon resigned the very day Altman was shooting at
the Grand Ole Opry, and when country music legend Roy Acuff
heard the news, he screamed at the cast 'look at what you've done

to our president!', and then locked himself in his dressing room and furiously played his fiddle.[2] Of course, the cast of *Nashville* was not directly responsible for Nixon's fall, but we might see Acuff as a stand-in for the Silent Majority and the weirdo longhairs and pot smokers on Altman's team as representative of the counterculture that Nixon's supporters blamed for the president's implosion. Notwithstanding the specificity of that moment, and the ephemera of clothing styles and hairdos, the characters of *Nashville* radiate as truly as authentic and imperfect people now as they did the first time I saw the film on a muddy VHS tape, circa 1991. It is the powerful *affect* the film engenders that stands the test of time, the way it allows viewers space to have positive or negative feelings for its flawed characters. The film offers no pure heroes or villains but, instead, people who occasionally do the right thing and often do the wrong thing. One character who is relentlessly kind, making no apparent ethical missteps, also suffers from what seems like an incurable nervous breakdown. Another particularly kind character is too trusting and is thus easily exploited. In Altman's world, to be gentle – especially if you are a woman – is to be vulnerable, and perhaps unhinged.

Nashville's flawed characters reflect a sensibility that permeated American films of the 1970s, when new directors such as Martin Scorsese, Paul Schrader, Brian DePalma and Francis Ford Coppola came from outside the studio system, bringing with them a taste for European art cinema, which they occasionally emulated, while also crafting their own style. A breakthrough book on these auteurs referred to them as *The Movie Brats*; they were welcome, if their output could be monetised by the studios, and irritating, because they had new ideas, which was an affront to an industry more comfortable with the tried-and-true than the novel. The book title was apt, but did not exactly apply to Altman, who was different, an outsider among outsiders. He had started out doing conventional stuff – industrial films and TV – and only later emerged as a 'new' upstart. He was born in 1925, and was solidly middle-aged when *Nashville* premiered. The point is worth emphasising because the 1970s was certainly an era of young innovators, but it also included a few somewhat older hands, like Alan J. Pakula and Sidney Lumet.

The films of the New Hollywood overlapped in their sensibilities. They were critical of American values, generally pessimistic, and often countercultural or liberal in their orientation. The films did not offer the kind of moral reassurance that the classic studio era had demanded. One poster for Scorsese's *Mean Streets* (1973) used the over-the-top tagline 'Go to church on Sunday, go to hell on Monday'. That exploitative line represented the opposite of the old Hollywood moral universe, which was shattered by the 1970s but had been cracking for twenty years under the weight of declining censorship norms and the rise of tough genres like film noir. Late 1960s pictures like *Bonnie and Clyde* (a 1967 studio production) and *Easy Rider* (a 1969 independent production) marked both the end of the old era and the beginning of something new. Over and over again, the breakthrough films of the 1970s offer characters caught up in forces beyond their control. They cannot win, solve the mystery, get the girl. If there's a villain, he probably won't get taken down (*The French Connection*, 1971). If he is taken down, it will be a hollow victory (*The Long Goodbye*, 1973; *Night Moves*, 1975). If the protagonist makes it through an adventure of self-discovery, the self that is discovered will not be a new, enlightened persona (*Five Easy Pieces*, 1970; *The King of Marvin Gardens*, 1972). He might get killed (*The Parallax View*, 1974), even if he doesn't 'deserve it', which could have justified the death of a protagonist thirty years earlier. Harry Caul of *The Conversation* (1974) is a surveillance expert (shades of Nixon and Watergate, obviously) who manages to solve a mystery and to survive physically, but he ends up under surveillance himself, and in a state of existential crisis. In *Bring Me the Head of Alfredo Garcia* (1974), Warren Oates as Bennie declares, 'Nobody loses all the time,' but that was just wishful thinking.

Anyone making a list of the breakthrough auteurs of the 1970s would rightly include Altman. His films of that era are peopled by losers facing very limited opportunities for personal enlightenment or clarity. The American Dream is not only kaput in his world, it was never really an option. This is all crucial context for understanding *Nashville* and Altman's place in the New Hollywood ecosystem. And yet the film stands apart from work by Altman's peers in at least three key ways.

First, it makes fewer commitments to narrative formulas. There's nothing confusing about the genre positioning of *The French Connection*, *The Godfather* (1972) or *Serpico* (1973). But what is *Nashville*? I've heard it referred to as a 'musical comedy', and it is true that the film contains numerous musical performances and a few humorous – albeit dark – moments. But it's not a musical in a conventional sense, or definitively an anti-musical. Most of *Nashville*'s characters have a relationship with the country music business, but the film largely sidesteps the genre elements one expects from a musical – the energy and joy of the numbers, the utopian feelings, the happy-ending-via-heterosexual-coupling, and so on. By contrast, Altman's *McCabe and Mrs. Miller* (1971) can reasonably be described as an anti-Western for its engagement with and re-envisioning of classic tropes – the expansion of 'civilisation' westward, the desire to strike it rich on the new frontier, the attempt at forging new community and, of course, the shootout. In the classic Western, the schoolmarm from the East represents a 'civilising force', what you might call 'wife material'. The dancehall girl, a thinly censored stand-in for the prostitute, represents the alternative. In the revisionist *McCabe and Mrs. Miller*, Shelley Duvall's mail-order-bride-turned-whore embodies these putative opposites.

The financial exploitation of '2-for-1 Lil' further underscores how human relations in *McCabe and Mrs. Miller* are inevitably tarnished by financial exchange. Yet, there is understated compassion here. Lil is heavy, and maybe understood as less valuable than the other prostitutes. But she markets herself as a good deal. She's making the best of things. *Nashville* likewise explores the ways that women deal with their own commodification, but not from the vantage point of genre commentary.

McCabe and Mrs. Miller (1971): Shelley Duvall's character is both wife and, later, prostitute; 2-for-1 Lil, whose name is literally her cost, underscores how the film lays bare human exploitation

Second, the film simply has too many characters and a meandering narrative trajectory. Even the darkest and most subversive New Hollywood films usually fell into the conventional formula of featuring a protagonist attempting to accomplish a goal, within a three-act structure of exposition, rising action, and finally climax and resolution. The resolution might be tenuous or indeterminate. Take, for example, Jerry Schatzberg's *Scarecrow* (1973), in which one character ends up catatonic and the other takes off, vaguely pledging to help his friend. The heroes have had adventures both good and bad together. One has been deeply harmed, and the other seems to have become a better person through friendship. The genre is clear – it's a buddy road movie. A studio executive might read the script and deem it incredibly depressing and, therefore, a surefire box-office dud (a correct evaluation, it turns out), but it would be legible as a film with linear character development and a coherent beginning, middle and end. When United Artists saw the original *Nashville* script, by contrast, their response, according to screenwriter Joan Tewkesbury, was 'This is a script?'[3] They dropped it. At that point, before Altman began to rework it, the film had eighteen characters and did not end with an assassination, but the uniquely meandering quality was there. Within the New Hollywood context, this movie was boldly amorphous.

And finally, *Nashville* stands apart from its New Hollywood peers for its explicit and conscious engagement with the issues of gender dynamics and gendered exploitation. As Molly Haskell argues in *From Reverence to Rape*, studio-era female characters were often powerful, funny and smart, but there was virtually no interest in such women in the masculinist new cinema of the 1970s, which offered mostly thankless roles to women.[4] Exceptions existed here and there. Ellen Burstyn brings memorable poignancy to *The King of Marvin Gardens*. Cloris Leachman and, again, Burstyn absolutely killed it in *The Last Picture Show* (1971), a film directed by Peter Bogdanovich but indelibly impacted by the creative decisions of his then wife Polly Platt, who influenced much more than the production

The Last Picture Show (1971) conveys atypical compassion for its female characters, such as sad Ruth Popper (Cloris Leachman) (John Springer Collection/Getty Images); mother and daughter Lois and Jacy Farrow (Ellen Burstyn and Cybill Shepherd) commiserate about men, the framing of the mirror symbolising their entrapment (Alamy)

design work for which she was credited.[5] Similarly, Tewkesbury's conceptualisation of *Nashville*, and of course the actors' brilliant improvisational performances, were crucial to conveying the nuances of the dysfunctional heterosexual relationships the film portrayed. It would be overly simplistic to describe the movie as 'feminist', but it does stand out for not *engaging* in comical misogyny, like Altman's earlier *M*A*S*H* (1970), instead *conveying* the pain and real damage of the exploitation of women.

And how was all of this received by critics and audiences? The film appeared to have strong box-office potential, pulling strong numbers in the big cities where it was initially released. It ultimately did not do well nationally. Having made a string of films that performed very poorly after *M*A*S*H*'s booming success in 1970, the 'success' of *Nashville* from the business angle was that it more than broke even. This was a tipping point moment when films were getting into many theatres quickly – 'saturation booking', as it was called in the business. At its height, *Jaws* (1975) played in 115 theatres. But *Nashville*, at its peak, hit only 27. Just a few years later, Altman's *A Perfect Couple* (1979) bombed, and *HealtH* (1980) was deemed wholly unreleasable, so *Nashville*'s relatively unimpressive box office was hardly a disaster in the context of Altman's financial ups and downs.[6]

Still, at one sour moment, Altman griped,

commercially, the biggest problem with the film is that it doesn't have a shark. So nobody really knows except by word of mouth, and somebody says 'You ought to see it, it's really good.' And you say 'What's it about?' And, well, you can't answer that. So that's the problem every time you do a film that doesn't have an absolute, *one* focal point.[7]

Obviously, lots of movies without sharks were struggling to compete financially in 1975, but of the top ten, four fit comfortably under the rubric of the New Hollywood – *One Flew Over the Cuckoo's Nest* (#2), *Shampoo* (#3), *Dog Day Afternoon* (#4) and *Three Days of the Condor* (#6). There was still room in the marketplace for weird, depressing, challenging movies in 1975, but not for *Nashville*, which was simply too experimental and sprawling, lacking not just the single heroic protagonist that the old Hollywood demanded but also the single doomed anti-hero common to the New Hollywood.

Critically, on the other hand, almost all the reviews were extremely positive. Altman often got rave reviews, not only because he made strong films, but also because he was good at courting attention from journalists, most famously the *New Yorker*'s Pauline Kael, who was privy to an advance screening of *Nashville*, to the consternation of other big-name reviewers. Altman took on interview after interview, and even when he came off looking like a jerk, the final article was good publicity for both him and his work. Aljean Harmetz profiled Altman for the *New York Times Magazine* during the shooting of *McCabe and Mrs. Miller*, and while her piece offers much insight into Altman's history and working style, it is the director's seemingly endless consumption of grass, Cutty Sark, red wine, white wine and hot buttered rum – not to mention his berating of Harmetz, his insistence upon driving drunk and his predilection for taking to bed to watch roller derbies on TV – that stands out in boldest relief. This was 'there's no such thing as bad publicity' stuff. Kael was his biggest booster, and her *Nashville* review was nothing short of rapturous. She captures the complexity of the film, its rhythm and its sprawling indeterminacy as a multi-character '*Grand Hotel*-style narrative … a country-and-western musical; a documentary essay on Nashville and American life; a meditation on the love affair between performers and audiences; and an Altman party'.[8] Kael is perhaps the reviewer who most deeply perceived the film as a comedy, 'the funniest epic vision of America ever to reach the screen'.

Kael might have been the most ebullient voice praising the picture, but the *New York Times* pulled out all the stops by reviewing and featuring the film over and over again. Vincent Canby praised it in a *Times* review on 12 June, the day after it opened. The next day, Paul Gardner wrote a piece touting the film, as per Altman, as

'a metaphor for my personal view of our society ... Nashville is the
new Hollywood, where people are tuned in by instant stars, instant
music, and instant politicians'.[9] A few days later in the Sunday
edition, Canby wrote about the film again on the front page of
the Arts and Leisure section, opposite an essay on the film by Tom
Wicker. Flipping to continue Canby's and Wicker's articles on
page 17, the reader passes a full-page *Nashville* ad on page 11; *Jaws*
(still to be released five days later) was the only other film to claim
an entire ad page. Keep going to pages 20 and 21 to encounter a big
spread for 'Korvettes Famous All Labels Sale! The World's Largest
Seller of Records and Tapes!', where the *Nashville* LP is advertised
for $4.29, billed above Pink Floyd. ABC Records hopefully declares:
'The Smash Hit Motion Picture of the Year Is Now a Smash Hit
Soundtrack'. That would seem to be plenty of publicity. But on
11 August the film opened in Nashville, and the *Times* fully covered
that event as well. Further, the day before the Nashville premiere,
the paper published an attack on the film by one John Malone, who
critiqued it as a misogynist monstrosity and simply too difficult
to understand. It was, Malone contended, 'vastly overpraised'.
Malone saw the film with an audience that laughed when characters
bottomed out, and he concluded that the problem was not a cruel
audience but a cruel film-maker.

Extra *Times* coverage is not uncommon for controversial
or historical movies like *The Last Temptation of Christ* (1988),
Schindler's List (1993) or *Saving Private Ryan* (1998). What put
Nashville in a league with those event films, at least in terms of media
buzz if not in terms of ticket sales? My hunch is that the answer is
twofold. First, the characters are compelling and beautifully acted,
and the film is visually stunning. In other words, it's great art. Second,
it struck a nerve when understood as a 'microcosm of America' at a
moment of ideological burnout.

The *Times* overkill coverage offers a tidy encapsulation of
the two sorts of reactions to the film. Either it was (or was not) an
epic masterpiece, or it was (or was not) an accurate political treatise

on America. Kael, Canby, Sarris, Haskell and many others came down on the masterpiece side, not ignoring the political angle but not taking it as their sole focus. On the political side, an inordinate number of non-film critics responded to the film. What was Tom Wicker doing reviewing alongside Vincent Canby? He was not a film critic but, rather, a political reporter, arguably the closest the *Times* came to embracing the New Journalism. He was the one who had been invited inside Attica prison as an observer by inmates who had seized the facility and held the guards hostage in 1971. Wicker's writing expressed political points of view, and he ended up on Nixon's list of enemies for his trouble. If *Nashville* was a takedown of Nixon's America, Wicker was a legitimate non-film reviewer to write on it; the subtitle of his piece says it all: 'A Cascade of Greed, Cruelty, Hysteria'.[10]

In Nashville itself, the response was mixed, ranging from negative to nonplussed. *Nashville*'s burn-victim-nervous-collapse centrepiece, Barbara Jean, was loosely based on country music star Loretta Lynn, who refused to watch the film. She declared that she'd rather watch *Bambi* (1942), and, further, that while it was quite fair for *Nashville* to show her having all kinds of breakdowns, because that was true to her life, her objection was that Altman killed her off at the end of the movie.[11]

The premiere was staged as a red-carpet event, with a crew of square dancers performing and four of the stars in attendance, along with local news reporter Bill Jenkins, who had appeared in the film as himself, acting as emcee. Local TV anchor (and 1972 Miss Black Nashville winner) Oprah Winfrey also covered the event. Following the screening, local reporters interviewed country music luminaries who had attended the premiere. Some found the film both funny and sad. Others were perplexed, or angered by what they judged to be poor music, which was understood as a bad reflection on the city's hot, growing industry. Grand Ole Opry icon Minnie Pearl tactfully described the movie as 'very interesting', while singer Ronnie Milsap said, 'I've seen a lot of movies in my day ... and this is one

The gala Nashville premiere of Altman's film included a performance by the Rutherford County Square Dancers (© 24800561 – Jimmy Ellis – USA TODAY NETWORK via Imagn Images); local TV newsman Bill Jenkins greets country music performers Ronnie Milsap and Jeanne Pruett (© 24899786 – Frank Empson – USA TODAY NETWORK via Imagn Images)

of them.'[12] It's quite likely Milsap would have offered a similar response following a screening of, say, *Five Easy Pieces*. That is, there's no reason to think that Altman's meandering film would have been embraced by local viewers not already interested in artsy films, even if the putative subject of *Nashville* was their hometown and their business. In fact, we would do well to remember that high grossers of the New Hollywood era included *The Aristocats* (1970), *Live and Let Die* (1973), *Benji* (1974) and *The Return of the Pink Panther* (1975). In 1975, at the peak of the New Hollywood, there was still a sizeable American audience looking for films that were not dark and difficult, especially in the politically conservative Bible Belt.

That said, there were a few hopeful signs for *Nashville* in *The Tennessean* newspaper. One letter to the editor, from the governor's office of Tourist Development, expresses amazement that anyone would find the film harmful, suggesting that just having the name of the city on marquees all over the country could only help boost the town, and concluding, 'I, for one, would be tremendously jealous if Robert Altman had made a movie titled *Atlanta*.'[13] Shortly before the film's New York City release, *The Tennessean* seemed to confirm this perspective with an article entitled 'Altman Goal: Crush Stereotype of South', in which the director explains, 'It is not a putdown. I have the greatest respect for Nashville and its music. If it's a putdown of anything, it's of me and my idea of what has happened to this country.'[14] These were not soothing words for Nashville citizens who disliked the film. It was, after all, a conservative city full of Nixon supporters. The president himself had visited to speak and play piano at the opening of the new Grand Ole Opry building in March 1974, where he played 'God Bless America' on the piano and assured his audience that country music 'does make America better'.[15] By the mid-1970s, country music was emerging as a symbolic cultural alternative to movies, or to put it more geographically, Nashville was emerging as an alternative to Hollywood for conservative media consumers.[16] Regardless of whether the bestselling musicians were actually conservative (John Denver, Willie Nelson and Linda

In March 1974, President Nixon attended the dedication of the new Grand Ole Opry building (David Hume Kennerly/ Getty Images)

Ronstadt all did very well with country albums in 1975), the *perception* that country music expressed the values of the Nixon era was gaining traction, so a film ostensibly about Nashville that was perceived as conveying Hollywood values was destined for rejection by the Right.

Like many in Nashville, conservative columnists George Will and Pat Buchanan unequivocally loathed the film. Indeed, Will and Buchanan are the best examples of the disgust exhibited by the minority of journalists who wrote negatively about *Nashville*, from the camp of pundits primarily interested in it as a commentary on America rather than as a work of art. Will opens by excoriating the reviews by Judith Crist, Kael and Wicker, who seem to revel in the film's attack on, as per Wicker,

a culture that does not even know it is choking on exhaust fumes ... a culture in which old people are thrown aside as carelessly as Colonel Sanders chicken bones, patriotism and sentimentality salve the hideous wounds of progress, and madmen peer mildly from benign eyes.[17]

Will's piece is entitled 'A Metaphor for America?', and his answer to that question is an emphatic 'no': the film is negative, facile and, above all, tacky. One character, he laments, clipped her toenails [*sic*] while her 'porcine' husband munched on fried chicken. Another character offered watermelon to a Black man at a stock car race, and some characters 'copulated non-stop in a motel'. To hear Will's description, you'd think *Nashville* was some kind of tawdry exploitation picture destined only for grindhouses and drive-ins. Worst of all, he states that the film 'is to America what country music is to music – not a close approximation'. Ouch. The one thing Will does get right, though, is his description of John Triplette: 'the operator whose activities thread other episodes together like beads ... [He] is a politician's advance man, central casting's idea of a Jeb Magruder look-alike'.[18] Nixon depended on 'plumbers' and 'ratfuckers', his men in charge of stopping leaks and executing dirty tricks. George Will was right to refer to *Nashville*'s manipulative political operative John Triplette as a sort of Jeb Magruder stand-in. Actor Michael Murphy had 'watched or read about every young lawyer who was involved in Watergate', Tewkesbury explained, and he clearly brought his knowledge of the president's 'ratfuckers' to his performance. Triplette brilliantly channelled a Nixon-operative tonal quality, as he successfully manipulated people to support presidential candidate Hal Phillip Walker.[19]

John Triplette was not the spitting image of Jeb Magruder, but George Will correctly intuited the character as an allusion to Nixon's minions (Bettmann/Getty Images)

This cynical political manoeuvring is at the heart of what makes the film, contra Will, a brilliant reflection of the American political scene. At the same time, Altman is offering a weird twist. In 1975, the very presence of a populist third-party candidate inevitably evoked George Wallace, the right-wing Alabama governor who had run on a third-party ticket in 1968 and who failed to be nominated on the Democratic ticket in 1972. He dropped out of the race following an assassination attempt in 1972. That year, the American Party, a spin-off of Wallace's American Independent Party, was running two John Birch Society members for president and vice president, affirming the generally understood connection at the time between third-party candidates and right-wingism. (Founded in 1958 and boosted by Barry Goldwater's 1964 presidential campaign, the anti-communist John Birch Society was for many years America's highest-profile conspiratorial organisation.) *Nashville*'s third-party candidate is a

★ ★ ★ ★ ★ ★ ★ ★ ★ ★ ★ ★ ★
STAND UP FOR AMERICA

LET THE PEOPLE SPEAK
★ ★ ★ ★ ★ ★ ★ ★ ★ ★ ★ ★ ★ ★ ★

Nashville's populist third-party political candidate, Hal Phillip Walker, leaned liberal and yet inevitably evoked George Wallace's failed campaigns (Alamy)

somewhat incoherent populist, certainly not a right-winger, and yet he is paired up with a publicity man who oozes Nixon vibes.

And this brings us to ratfucker Patrick Buchanan, a White House aide, speechwriter and Nixon loyalist to the bitter end, whose write-up (given the lack of close engagement with the film, one hesitates to call it a 'review') was entitled '"Nashville" is Slander on Celluloid'. Unlike Will, Buchanan acknowledges the film as an Oscar-worthy artistic achievement, but he cannot forgive its anti-American cynicism. Moreover, he suggests that Altman is part of a 'thoroughly jaded artistic and intellectual community, which has grown rich and gains its amusement by mocking the good society and system which guarantees the freedom it so regularly abuses'.[20]

This sounds like any number of speeches that Buchanan authored for former Vice President Spiro T. Agnew (forced to resign in disgrace almost two years before Buchanan's column appeared), minus the irritating alliteration of phrases like 'nattering nabobs of negativism'. Buchanan specialised in attacking elites and intellectuals and, in particular, the American news media. For him, Altman is just a different version of CBS anchorman Walter Cronkite – more pessimistic, more artistic, but equally liberal and anti-American. In the years to come, Buchanan would build a media and political career on right-wing, anti-Semitic, anti-gay, anti-immigration rhetoric. As a candidate running for president in the 1990s, Buchanan was so purely right-wing one could not imagine him in an Altman film; the character would be too obvious, beyond satire.[21]

Nixon's man Pat Buchanan would later run for president himself, leaning hard into anti-immigration bigotry (Chris Wilkins/AFP/Getty Images)

Like Will, Buchanan perceives Triplette as *Nashville*'s throughline, describing him as 'an amoral, low-keyed, seersuckered political advance man'. Any thoughtful viewer of the film would understand Triplette as amoral; the question, then, is how does one feel about that amorality? Altman's stance on Triplette is perhaps less evaluative than realist: this is simply what American politics looks like, for better or for worse. The whole point of this character, of course, is that even though he's working for a third-party candidate, not the Republicans, he specifically embodies the Nixonian dark side of the film. In July 1973, Buchanan had sent Nixon a memo specifically advising him to destroy his secretly made tapes.[22] Triplette would no doubt have suggested the same.

All in all, most reviewers loved the film, a few political journalists hated it, New York and Los Angeles art crowd audiences flocked to it, the Nashville audience was spare and dour, and it never reached the box-office peaks that many other New Hollywood films achieved. While *Nashville* shared the dark perspective of the cinema of losers, it stood out from the pack for its peripatetic structure and over-the-top cast size. The question that remains, then, is how on earth did Altman come to make this wild film, so unconventional even by the standards of 1970s American cinema?

2 From 'The Perfect Crime' to 'Grand Motel'

Altman once called *Nashville* his 'Grand Motel', a play on the title of MGM's 1932 *Grand Hotel*. The line was not entirely a joke. *Grand Hotel* was an overwrought classic, extravagantly cast with too many stars to work, in theory. But work it did, as did *Nashville*, with its own excessive casting and sprawling sets of relationships. If you stretch the analogy and squint a little, you might say that Altman and Tewkesbury switched out John Barrymore for Keith Carradine and Joan Crawford for Lily Tomlin. (Or Greta Garbo for Ronee Blakley, both playing unhinged divas.) And there you have it: with two classic silver screen actors who oozed sophistication and sex appeal replaced by a lanky and scruffy kid in his second leading American film role and a wonky-looking TV comedy star, the Grand Hotel had become a Motel 6.

The analogy only takes one so far, however. For one thing, *Grand Hotel* was made by Edmund Goulding, a director from the classic studio era. Altman started making features as the studio system took its final gasps, and he had no roots in that system. Many of the New Hollywood actors and directors – Scorsese, Coppola, Jack Nicholson, Peter Fonda – got their start working on exploitation films with Roger Corman in California. Altman, conversely, began his career in industrial film-making at the Calvin Company in Kansas City, Missouri, in the 1950s. This work made him efficient and conditioned him to limited budgets. He could perform any technical job on any shoot, he claimed, and it was probably true.

Calvin was a successful, reputable company that made industrial films for screening at workplaces and in schools. Topics ranged from tactics for selling more tyres at service stations to explaining the rules of football. Such for-hire, utilitarian films did not require high-quality acting or aesthetic innovation, and they did not depend upon ticket sales. Altman's later career, of course, rested upon just the opposite: innovation in acting and improvisation, a unique approach to sound and image, and ups and down at the box office. Altman both fitted in and stood out at Calvin. He was more curious about sound design than was typical, and he had a few technologically innovative ideas. Calvin directors (who also often scripted and edited their own films) shot sound-on-film dialogue rather than crafting separate dialogue and image recordings that would enable more flexibility in post-production. Music and voiceovers were added in post, and some Calvin films had little or no dialogue. This was a cheap and efficient approach to film-making. Altman mixed it up by looping dialogue for a 1950 Calvin film called *Honeymoon for Harriet*. In Hollywood this was standard practice, but at Calvin adding dialogue in post-production was like inventing the wheel. Altman also favoured location shooting and moved the camera more than some of his peers.[23] Calvin's loose understanding of scripts as flexible blueprints was not uncommon in industrial films, but it was rare in conventional Hollywood film-making. Altman would later lean into this hard, allowing wide latitude for his actors to improvise.

One errs in trying to trace a direct aesthetic or political line from Altman's work at Calvin to his Hollywood films, and more specifically to *Nashville*. For one thing, there's no definitive Calvin filmography, and the list of films we know were directed by Altman may be incomplete. And yet ... there is resonance. Industrial films are often wonky, disconcerting or even inadvertently avant-garde, and Altman spent almost a decade making these sorts of films. That sometimes joyous feeling of 'what the hell am I watching?' tugs at the curious viewer of industrial films, or at least tugs at the feelings of this viewer.

Industrial and educational films are often boring and unwatchable, but when they do pull us in, it is through the fortuitous, unexpected genius of incompetence that comes from a director making a film without proper training or from using comically bad actors. The impact of these weird little movies depends heavily on viewing environment. Michael Murphy, who plays political operative John Triplette in *Nashville*, recounted in an interview with me the strong impression that *USS VD: Ship of Shame* (1942) had had on him. The film advocates condom use by positioning women as little more than disease carriers, and includes a graphic depiction of a ravaged male sex organ. Murphy had seen the picture in Marine boot camp but could describe it in extremely vivid detail, some sixty years later. Context is all. An awkward 1950s 16mm menstruation film will impact high-school students in the throes of puberty differently than it will adult film buffs watching a tattered old Something Weird VHS tape of the film decades later. You might watch a hundred wonky instructional or educational films and never have some sort of eureka moment, but if you do, it comes with a sense of wonder that a boring film about how to apply make-up, or reduce the number of time-consuming coffee breaks your employees are taking, or avoid getting the clap, can be strangely shocking or moving. It is the awkward comedy or drama of the mundane that enthrals.

Altman's feature-film work likewise taps into this sort of awkward mundanity. Consider *California Split* (1974). Why watch two men sing and talk and gamble and flirt and eat cereal and smoke cigarettes, in a film that is sort of about gambling but ignores most conventional notions of how to build a story to a climax? In one pathetic but poignant scene, Bill (George Segal) and Charlie (Elliott Gould) settle in for a breakfast-of-losers: Budweiser, Lucky Charms,

California Split (1974) privileges the mundane

cigarettes, Froot Loops, and for ambiance in the foreground, a plate of old victuals that Charlie refers to as 'paté de foie garbage'. In a film with minimal narrative, a mundane scene like this stands out for building not story but character. At the end, one of our 'heroes', Bill, has a big lucky streak at gambling, and then has an epiphanic moment as his friend Charlie tries to bundle up the jackpot in his shoes: 'There was no special feeling.' Charlie tries to boost his mood, but then ultimately agrees: 'It don't mean a fucking thing, does it?' I could have told him that two hours ago! But I'm glad I hung out with him while he figured it out. Is this also the ending of *Nashville*? Does what we have just witnessed not mean a fucking thing? How could a crowd of country music fans, having seen their favourite star assassinated, join in with a tattered would-be superstar in ripped stockings to sing 'It Don't Worry Me'? Yes, the murder is meaningless, if you take the words at face value, but I think not, because it all *does* mean something.

Even if Altman's early Calvin films are most emphatically not works of hidden genius offering a magic key to understanding the director, they do help to situate some of the feelings evoked by his later work, and they help us situate how he made his way to *Nashville*. Take Altman's violent yet boring road safety film *The Perfect Crime* (1955), which opens with a robbery and double murder, followed by an arrest, all in the first three minutes. We appear to be watching a heist film. But then the next seventeen minutes centre on the notion of the 'perfect crime', starting with a car accident in which a man survives but his wife and child die. A stern narrator instructs us that this 'accident' was actually 'murder' because it was caused by a road in poor repair. The film is relentlessly depressing, as the roadside corpses (apparently staged with actors) pile up, and the narrator predicts death at every twist and turn in the road regardless of car condition, speed limits or driver sobriety. 'I killed them, you helped,' the narrator concludes in the big twist ending: it is he who accidentally murdered his own wife and child in the second scene of the film. *The Perfect Crime* is restrained compared to so many driver safety films packed with gory documentary images. Further, such films usually instruct viewers, often presumed to be young and impressionable, not to drink or speed. *The Perfect Crime*, by contrast, suggests that letters to politicians might help improve road quality, but that the whole situation is basically hopeless. The negativity feels like trademark Altman, although without the lighter moments of humour offered in many of his later films.

Altman's Calvin film *The Magic Bond* (1956), commissioned to promote the Veterans of Foreign Wars (VFW), is much more upbeat and solutions-oriented than *The Perfect Crime*, but it too opens with a conventional genre set-up (the war film) before switching to a didactic mode. Calvin's internal guidelines discussed the challenges (and pitfalls) of such entertaining 'Big Openings',[24] so it's not that Altman's Calvin productions were kooky by industrial film standards but, rather, that he cut his teeth making films with moments of genre indeterminacy. His heist films were not heist films. His war films were not war films. Later in his feature work, sci-fi films were not sci-fi films (*Countdown*, 1967), Westerns were not Westerns (*McCabe and Mrs. Miller*) and, in the case of *Nashville*, musicals were not musicals.

Industrial films were purposeful and efficient, usually hewing to problem–solution formulas. Need better tyres? Buy this brand. Unpopular with boys? Try better soap. *The Magic Bond* establishes juvenile delinquency, apathy towards political challenges and neglect of veterans as problems, and then shows how VFW projects offer solutions, all of which will make us stronger in our battle against the Commies. The film seems to confirm without irony that we have indeed been doing something right to last two hundred years – exactly the sort of patriotism and can-do spirit that is ironised and undermined in the opening scene of *Nashville*, and even obliquely in *Countdown*. Except Altman includes archival footage of a VFW marbles competition in which a Black boy plays alongside a white boy. That's a remarkable choice, but it is, after all, a documentary record of something that happened, whether viewers liked it or not. A later moment feels more deliberately confrontational.

As a Black child sits down to dinner with white children, the voiceover explains that the VFW helps children who have lost their fathers to be 'integrated into a normal family life'. The narrator puts hard emphasis on the word 'integrated'. It's the sort of detail that points to a liberal sensibility, and one that Calvin's client, VFW, might well not have shared.

In 1956, a Kansas City businessman hired Altman to make *The Delinquents* (1957), starring Tom Laughlin, later of *Billy Jack* (1971) fame. Shot on a shoestring $60,000 budget, the wobbly film was no masterpiece, but it got picked up by United Artists. Altman's agent showed it to Hitchcock, who hired Altman to work on the TV series *Suspicion* (1957–8), and then, briefly, *Alfred Hitchcock Presents* (1955–62). From there, Altman moved on to *Combat!* (1962–7) (including a 1963 episode with Murphy, one of the first *Nashville* actors to enter Altman's universe) and other shows. The director now had an opportunity to produce commercially appealing material written and produced by others, in a context where technical independence was still undervalued, but above-average acting was desirable. Altman would later become known for his keen interest in approaching scripts as outlines more than bibles, and for his promotion of on-set improvisation, the last thing that was desirable in Hollywood TV studios, where weekly series efficiently reused characters and situations precisely to streamline and economise production. This was not to Altman's taste, though he had steady work and earned a large salary. When Warner Bros. offered him *Countdown* in 1967, he jumped on it. It would be his first studio picture, a foot in the door enabled by ten years of competent TV work.

The raging success of *M*A*S*H* in 1970, plus support from Twentieth Century Fox head of production Alan Ladd Jr, whom Altman playfully called 'Laddie', kept the studios financing Altman's films throughout the 1970s in the hope that he might strike gold again. He did not. But he *did* consistently come in on budget, and this is key to understanding how Altman got from Calvin to *Nashville*. The director was eccentric by Hollywood standards in terms of casting, scripts, sound and editing choices – everything really. But he could keep to a schedule. The *fiscal discipline* of working on industrial films and TV shows in his early years made Altman's bumpy and otherwise eccentric career viable. He definitely lied to the suits in management all the time, affirming, for example, that he would shoot a scene or stick to an ending as written in the script, but he didn't lie about how much it would all cost or when he would finish the final cut.

M*A*S*H's importance to Altman's career from the commercial and technical standpoint was twofold: he premiered his eight-track recording system, bolstering his innovations in improvisation and overlapping dialogue, which would reach a new crescendo with *Nashville*; and the film earned the third highest US box-office gross of 1970. But the story of Altman's path to his 1975 masterpiece must be one of meaning, not just money. And to my mind, the pressing, gnawing centre of *Nashville* is the laying bare of the suffering of women. A number of his early films help track Altman's journey in this direction: *The Model's Handbook* (1956), *Countdown*, *That Cold Day in the Park* (1969), *Images* (1972) and *Thieves Like Us* (1974).

Sponsored by the Ford Modeling Agency, *The Model's Handbook* feels very much like a Calvin instructional film, but it was created as a TV pilot, back when fifteen minutes was still a common length for low-profit programming such as news and public affairs, or low-prestige shows such as soap operas and exercise or cooking lessons, material patently targeting women. *The Model's Handbook* opens with mildly salacious shots of a lady walking up a flight of stairs in seamed stockings, followed by a bit of chaos at the agency's telephone bank – a taste of Altman's overlapping dialogue – before moving on to an instructional segment on posture exercises offered by supermodel Dorian Leigh, in a zippered leotard performing light calisthenics. A female narrator explains: 'The basis of all true beauty is good health, and you just can't be healthy if your posture's bad … Perfect posture demands a flat tummy … Without proper diet, all the exercise in the world is wasted.' This is classic, normative gender instruction, although Leigh was a rather extraordinary woman, thirty-nine years old when she appeared in Altman's film (an old crone by modelling standards) and a free spirit, reportedly part inspiration for Truman Capote's Holly Golightly.[25] Oddly enough, there was a strange *Nashville* connection, as Leigh had met Geraldine Chaplin's father, Charlie, in Switzerland in 1955, having escaped abroad to bear a secret love child. Be that as it may, *The Model's Handbook* was as conventional as its star was unconventional. Altman was not interested here in bending or breaking the norms of genre or gender. We might take this as the baseline of Altman presenting gender norms in an achingly conventional manner.

A decade later, *Countdown* offers a radically different perspective. In Altman's hands, the astronaut movie, one of the most male genres, teeters between displaying masculine bravado and female conformity and, if not overtly critiquing, at least exposing the cracks in both postures. Robert Duvall and James Caan play Chiz and Lee, duelling macho astronauts, with Joanna Moore as Mickey, Lee's nauseatingly supportive wife. Critics declared it an utter bore at the time, and when the Harvard Film Archive curated a programme of Altman's features in 2015, they described it simply as a for-hire B-movie. If the viewer expects a standard astronaut movie with lots of action and terrific special effects, the production is definitely flawed. Instead, *Countdown* offers stock footage of rockets launching, a poor simulation of the moon's surface, and, most importantly, couples and bureaucrats arguing and cajoling one another – what actually happens in marriages in daily life, and at NASA on the vast majority of days when they don't send a rocket up. The film is not an exciting space adventure but, rather, a chronicle of NASA stupidly choosing to send an unqualified civilian (Lee/Caan) to the moon to prove that American space travel is not a military operation. It's simply a bureaucratic murder/suicide plan to demonstrate US superiority to the Russians. Learning of the doomed mission, fellow astronaut Rick (Murphy) asks a patently unpatriotic question: 'Who thought it up, an LSD research team?'

The wives suffer. Barbara Baxley (later Lady Pearl in *Nashville*) drunkenly circles the room as the menfolk discuss the doomed mission. Lee's wife Mickey offers loving support, chirpily exclaiming, 'If you're happy, I'm happy!' and 'If Lee says we are going to the moon, we are going to the moon, until Lee says we are not going to the moon!' Things go awry, however, when she realises the true dangers of the mission: 'If you knew all these things all along, you were lying like hell to me, weren't you? ... Lee, what happened to all the caution you promised me? What do you expect me to do? Smile?' Lee explodes: 'Yeah, you smile. You got that? Hmm? *If it kills you, you just smile*. SMILE!' He then puts his arm around her neck, in a gesture that signals either affection or the opposite. The scene ends abruptly, which happens more than once, probably because Altman was fired after he shot the film, and the studio cut its own version, tacking on a highly improbable happy ending.[26]

What is moving in this truncated scene is the sudden brutality and, ultimately, the truth in the Lee–Mickey relationship. Lee doesn't always treat his wife well, reminding one of the troubled relationships of *Nashville*, especially Barnett attacking his wife Barbara Jean with a question to which he desires no answer: 'Are you THROUGH?' But several moments of tenderness also stand out in *Countdown*, most strikingly a bedroom scene, in which Lee and Mickey discuss their worries, their bodies (fully clothed) inverted head-to-toe. They take a moment of silence. Lee flicks Mickey's behind with his hand in a sort of weird, 'hey, kiddo, love you' type of gesture. She reaches up, and he reaches down, and they clasp hands, the shot framed to show their hands and inverted midriffs. These intimate gestures don't solve the problems in their relationship. Mickey is a helpmate, taking all the personality flaws that Lee dishes out. At one point, Lee desperately asks Mickey, 'If I don't make this trip, then who the hell am I, Mick? Forgive me. Forgive me.' If he declines the mission, he won't be a real man. This flawed film anticipates some of the most poignant moments between men and women in the infinitely more sophisticated *Nashville*.

Frances in *That Cold Day in the Park* (1969), gazes at the young man who will become the object of her obsession, the fence between them an obvious marker of her alienation

Images and *That Cold Day in the Park* also pursue the problems of male–female relationships, and how women deal with the crisis of their own oppression. The films are dire, showing trapped women and offering homicide as perhaps inevitable. *Cold Day*, in particular, demands we understand its protagonist, Frances (Sandy Dennis), as a woman desperately attempting to seize control of her destiny. In one standout scene, a much older man attempts to pressure Frances into a sexual relationship, the sort of intergenerational romance normalised and presented as highly desirable for women in so many Hollywood films, but here clearly framed as repellent. The protagonist flashes back to her trip to the OB/GYN earlier in the day, where, in order to get an IUD, she lied that she was 'about to get married', as other women in the office engaged in frank gynaecological discussion. With the exception of outright feminist alternative film-making of the 1970s, one would be hard-pressed to find a more sharply focused picture of women of that era dealing with these sorts of personal issues, even as the film closes out with a bizarre prostitute murder that is no triumph for the women's movement.

Thieves Like Us, Joan Tewkesbury's first script before *Nashville*, offers up what I would guardedly call a 'successful' heterosexual relationship, between two simple, scrawny Depression-era kids who love Coca-Cola, sex and listening to the radio. Their love is true, like a Romeo and Juliet radio play, and just as doomed. Bowie (Keith Carradine) and Keechie (Shelley Duvall) are able to

Thieves Like Us (1974): equally young and innocent, Keechie and Bowie discover lovemaking together; a darker vision of the Depression than *Bonnie and Clyde* (1967)

connect precisely because they are so young and naïve. It's as if they haven't matured enough to grasp the inevitable troubles inherent in heterosexual relations. In counterpoint to *Bonnie and Clyde*, with its gorgeous movie stars slaughtered in slow motion, *Thieves Like Us* ends with an even more baldly realistic and meaningless massacre. Bowie is assassinated by hundreds of bullets shot through the wall of his hideout, and with no reaction shots from the inside, Altman emphasises the impersonality of the murder; his body is dumped in the mud, wrapped in the same blanket that once covered the young lovers. Keechie is left pregnant and alone.

It would be impossible to do justice in a few pages to *3 Women* (1977), a complex film that follows *Nashville*, but even a quick look reveals a deep perspective on the toll that women pay just for being women – a theme that climaxes with the later film but is indebted to the groundwork laid in Altman's preceding films, especially *Nashville*. It is exactly the protagonist Millie's (Shelley Duvall)

Again in 3 Women (1977), Altman uses a fence to indicate female disconnection and alienation. Pinky Rose (Sissy Spacek) is on the outside looking in

Millie strikes a pose

obsessive collection of recipe cards and attempts to assimilate to conventional norms that is her undoing. She's the target audience for *The Model's Handbook*, a skinny gal who'd love to slip into a bright yellow leotard and smoke a menthol cigarette while doing some bust exercises. Millie seems to say all the right words, but she just can't perform femininity properly, and always seems to be rehearsing that persona rather than genuinely inhabiting it. For this crime, most around her express cold contempt as she attempts flirtation and small talk. Some people just can't pull off these sorts of ineffable, gendered charades. *3 Women* is Duvall's masterpiece, and a film with wholly different ambitions than *Nashville*. As L.A. Joan, the actress gets much less to do, as she wanders through *Nashville* in constantly changing outfits and wigs, with minimal dialogue. And yet that significantly less-developed character is still heartbreaking. L.A. Joan does so much with so little, and in a way this sums up all the women in *Nashville*. One must make do with life's constant disappointments, the fact that one 'never gets enough', as Sueleen Gay (Gwen Welles) sings, with a voice that reverberates like ground glass.

Like L.A. Joan, *Nashville*'s Albuquerque (Barbara Harris) has also renamed herself. The flipside of the ever-striving-for-propriety Millie, Albuquerque sleeps in abandoned cars and is dishevelled, mumbly and strange. She's fled her husband to get into country music, but if that doesn't work, she's fully prepared and qualified to go into auto sales or maintenance, even though she's been told that men are not interested in buying cars from girls. She's not trim because she's been dieting or doing posture exercises but because she doesn't have a dime to her name. Late in the film, Albuquerque shows up at a smoker – a men's stag event – disconcertingly peering through the curtains, gnawing on a turkey leg like some kind of sitcom Henry VIII parody, not because she's interested in watching a strip show, but because she's scrounging free food.

But the film doesn't exactly explain this. And this brings us to screenwriter Joan Tewkesbury, who in an interview explains that a sign marked 'benefit' on the street outside the smoker clued Albuquerque that there was probably free food on offer, a detail that was shot but left out of the film's final cut.[27] After Tewkesbury wrote the script, Altman and the actors brought their own ideas to the table and made changes. Here's how she explains her creative process:

Some people are great storytellers, like off the top of their head they can sit over the kitchen table and tell you this story that breaks your heart. I'm like a vacuum cleaner and so my craft really involves circling and getting a lot of information and then ... It's like cooking: You try some of this and you try some of that until you have order. Order is really important. Bob and I talked a lot, but he was shooting *Thieves* when I went to Nashville the first time, and then he shot another film. And so I just kept adding characters and then he added the political line and the assassination and we sort of went from there. Polly Platt quit because she hated the assassination. She was going to [do the film's] production design.[28]

There are a few remarkable things here. First, the references to cooking and housekeeping implicitly position Tewkesbury's labour as female, giving 'women's work' the most positive connotation imaginable. Second, Platt hated the final murder enough to walk away from the whole project. It was cruel to kill the beautiful and fragile Barbara Jean, like stomping on a baby bird. I don't believe that Altman did it out of misogyny, but it's quite possible that Platt read it that way. And finally, Altman's addition of the political angle is crucial, with the inclusion of Replacement Party candidate Hal Phillip Walker as a throughline. That revision helped viewers intuitively understand the film as relevant to the Watergate moment, situating it as an overt political commentary on America. But Platt's walkout reminds us that 'politics' are not just about candidates and elections. As per the feminist dictum, 'the personal is political'.

Tewkesbury recounts that ABC ultimately took a gamble on funding *Nashville* because they liked the script, but they hedged their bets, rationalising that 'they could also make a record deal, which meant that if the movie fell on its ass, they could recoup any loss by the sale of the record'.[29] That was not an accurate prediction. But it does perhaps indicate that ABC (and Paramount, who distributed) weren't sure of the film's potential. This was before *Saturday Night Fever* (1977) had made a fortune on soundtrack sales. That anyone would move forward with the *Nashville* script on the tenuous notion that maybe the LP would make it worthwhile points to how bonkers the whole greenlighting process was in the mid-1970s, and how desperate studios were for a *M*A*S*H*-level hit.

Riding the success of *M*A*S*H*, and building on a number of films that had reflected critically on both American politics and the ups and downs (but mostly downs) of heterosexual relationships, Altman took his wry cynicism to the next level with *Nashville*. It was anti-Nixon, anti-cruelty, anti-establishment and anti-bullshit, all the while realising that Nixon, cruelty, the establishment and bullshit were just realities that were not going away. 'Life may be a one-way street', but what other options do we have?

3 'All the World is Taking Sides, But It Don't Worry Me'

Nashville began as a Nixon film and ended as a Ford film. Shooting began in July 1974, and Nixon resigned in August. Thus, the film was released in 1975 with a new president in office and a pardoned Nixon in retreat in San Clemente. Nixon's name is never spoken in the film, even as Watergate hangs in the air. He appears briefly on a poster in a bar (wearing roller skates!) and is referred to as 'the asshole' in the course of one character's rant about the assassination of the Kennedy boys. Rather than attacking the disgraced Republican or boosting the idea that a Democrat might do a better job in the White House, *Nashville* offers a third-party, populist presidential candidate, Hal Phillip Walker, as an audio thread running through the film, as it wanders from character to character. He's campaigning as the candidate for the Replacement Party. A pathetic name for a political party? Satirical? Yes, both. Gerald Ford was a Republican but would also become the elliptical butt of the joke: he's the first Replacement Party president.

Walker never mentions Nixon (or Agnew, already ejected from office when Altman started shooting) because the film's perspective is too cynical to imply that replacing one guy with another would fix America's problems. The idea of 'replacement' is promoted, but there's nothing that makes Walker seem like someone with big ideas who will make a difference. He's against lawyers being in politics. He thinks the national anthem is a poor song that should be replaced by a tune with easier-to-remember lyrics. He's probably more liberal than conservative, because he advocates taxing churches, but he also wants to eliminate farm subsidies. The very presence of a third-party candidate would have resonated in 1975 as an allusion to George Wallace, but Walker, whose dialogue was all scripted by its performer, liberal Mississippian

THE PRESIDENT'S RECORD-PLUS A GIANT FOLD-OUT POSTER FOR YOUR WALL

Nixon captured nearly half the ballots of young, first-time voters in 1972 (Kean Collection/Getty Images)

Thomas Hal Phillips, pointedly avoids discussion of 'state's rights' or 'busing', dog whistles for segregationists. In fact, when Altman hired Phillips he told him he could conceive the Walker persona however he wanted, as long as he was a third-party candidate who he (Phillips) thought both could and should be elected. Walker is more populist than anything else – not hateful like Wallace, but echoing the folksy style Wallace often used. College students have been supporting him, which seems to be a vague reference to failed 1968 peace candidate Eugene McCarthy, but Nixon was swept into office in 1972 with support from Young Voters for the President, and he had lowered the voting age to eighteen. By 1975, being a college kid did not guarantee you would back a progressive candidate.

The first scene of the film opens with Walker's voice emanating from a travelling sound truck. 'New Roots for the Nation' is the meaningless slogan atop his vehicle, and the slogan on his campaign headquarters garage door reads 'WALKER•TALKER•SLEEPER', which is, let's face it, the baseline for most human beings. Walker's image is never shown, which in a way is the most politically radical statement the film makes. In a political world where visual image is key, a fact relentlessly exploited by Nixon and his image wranglers,[30] *Nashville* pretends that a faceless candidate could actually exist. Nixon won not only through dirty tricks like planting fake letters-to-the-editor in newspapers and otherwise sabotaging his rivals, but also by selling himself like Coca-Cola. He was the 'New Nixon' in 1968,

In 1971, Nixon tries to look relaxed by staging a photo op at the sea
(Bettmann/Getty Images)

like an improved floor wax. In 1971 he staged a photo op in which
he strolled on the beach in a windbreaker, to show himself in a casual
light. The stunt backfired because he was wearing wingtips. He knew
his visual image was important to his political success, but it was a
constant struggle. Hal Phillip Walker, by contrast, is a faceless presence.
You might vote for him because you agree that lawyers are elitists,
but you won't vote for him because he's got a great smile and a strong
hairline. He's not the real thing, but he's also not the Real Thing.

The film closes at a campaign rally for Walker that is cut short
by an assassination – not of him but of country music star Barbara
Jean. Barbara Jean is the other thread running through the film, not
the protagonist, as there is no single main character, but the one
who a number of other characters converge around or diverge from.
She's a sort of magnet by virtue of her talent and celebrity. The film
is dubious about the value of stardom in America, where everybody
wants his or her fifteen minutes in the spotlight, à la Andy Warhol,
but the biggest star in the film actually *is* a wonderful singer. She's
successful not only because she's beautiful and has a ruthless manager
(her husband Barnett) but also because she is talented.

Over the film's five days, Barbara Jean has a spotlight moment every day, and that's part of the glue that holds the whole wild production together. That said, it would be too pat to say that she's the centrepiece. Some characters have little or no interest in her. Still, along with Walker's peripatetic voice, she helps the film cohere, and it's useful for a newcomer to *Nashville* to keep this in mind while trying to navigate Altman's overwhelming production. I suspect that some reviewers pointed to political operative John Triplette as the film's throughline in an attempt to make the picture seem more normal and comprehensible: a male protagonist seeking political success is a standard Hollywood plotline, but *Nashville* does not take this kind of straightforward, linear approach.

Asked once if he had been influenced by Hitchcock, Altman replied, 'I've never been a big Hitchcock fan. His films are really too linear for me.'[31] It takes chutzpah for a director to reject the work of someone as lionised as Hitchcock. He wasn't too keen on Orson Welles, either. This all makes sense in light of Altman's improvisatory approach to narrative and character development. When I asked Michael Murphy what films Altman liked beside his own, the only one he could recall was Pasolini's *The Gospel According to St. Matthew* (1964), because it was so goddamn grotty, so many flies! This disconcerting Jesus was the opposite of Hollywood's cleaned-up version. Of course, Altman watched a vast number of films, and was particularly keen on Bergman and Fellini, but was also deeply versed in classical Hollywood cinema. He preferred the unconventional, non-linear European approach, but he also understood exactly how more conventional films worked, like a jazz musician who can perform off book precisely because he or she so clearly understands what it means to perform on book.

If *Nashville* is 'linear' at all, it's only in terms of chronology: it starts on Friday and ends on Tuesday. Barbara Jean does exert a sort of gravitational pull that powers *Nashville*, but that alone is not enough to direct a first-time viewer. In fact, Altman expected that films of quality, including his own, had to be seen at least a second time to be grasped. He was puzzled that no one would find it strange to listen to the same album or view the same painting repeatedly, yet somehow it seemed absurd to expect someone to buy a second ticket to a film.[32]

Part of what overwhelms the novice *Nashville* viewer is the sheer number of characters, as shown in the table below. What may immediately stand out is that although I've described him as a 'thread', Hal Phillip Walker is not actually a character. He's a quick refrain recurring in a much more complicated melody of characters. Although the common wisdom is that *Nashville* has twenty-four characters, that's a stretch, as some of them are barely developed and have few or even no lines. In the table, I've grouped the characters by relationship where possible, highlighting the most important figures in bold.

Character (Actor)	Description
Haven Hamilton (Henry Gibson)	Vain and self-serving Nashville singing star. He's powerful, he knows it and he'd like to be more powerful.
Lady Pearl (Barbara Baxley)	Initially appears to be Haven's wife but is actually his lover. Obsessed with the assassinated Kennedy boys. She's frequently loud and drunk, a sad character meant to offer both pathos and comic relief.
Bud Hamilton (Dave Peel)	Milquetoast son of Haven Hamilton. He's displayed on stage at Nashville's Grand Ole Opry so Haven can show he made a son. Remains an underdeveloped character.
Tom Frank (Keith Carradine)	Part of the Bill, Mary and Tom singing trio, a folk-rock band visiting Nashville. Tom is the object of desire of multiple women. He sleeps with many, with no emotional commitments. He's callous but too self-absorbed to be deliberately villainous. He just doesn't care.
Mary (Cristina Raines)	Part of the Bill, Mary and Tom singing trio, sad wife of Bill, sleeping with Tom, to whom she expresses her love over and over again … while he dozes.
Bill (Allan Nicholls)	Part of the Bill, Mary and Tom singing trio, husband of Mary. The character remains largely undeveloped.

Character (Actor)	Description
Connie White (Karen Black)	Star singer, rival to Barbara Jean. Offers superficial friendliness to fans and seems an unkind person at heart. At times the character is used to lampoon celebrity, as when she engages in phoney stage banter.
Barbara Jean (Ronee Blakley)	Hugely successful singer. Suffers from nervous breakdowns; she is fragile and was recently hospitalised for burn treatment. People are drawn to her both because she is a star and because she is talented. Although some of the songs written for the film are weak, viewers shouldn't glibly presume that Altman is attacking country music as junk when he's cast a clearly talented singer as the biggest star in town.
Barnett (Allen Garfield)	Husband and business manager to Barbara Jean. Protective of her, yet also abusive. He's got a short fuse.
Mr Green (Keenan Wynn)	His wife is dying. He thinks of little else. Why has he brought his uncaring niece to visit her in hospital?
L.A. Joan (Shelley Duvall)	Mr Green's visiting niece, always on the make, always changing her appearance with wigs and skimpy clothes. Is she wildly confident or wildly insecure?
Sueleen Gay (Gwen Welles)	Excruciatingly poor singer who wants to be a star. Wrenchingly exploited in a pivotal scene that stands out, arguably, as the smartest commentary on gendered exploitation in any film of the era.
Wade (Robert Doqui)	Works at the airport diner with Sueleen. Comes to her rescue at a key moment. Tries to pick up an unresponsive Linnea. Tries to pick a fight with Tommy Brown – the film's other Black character – for being a 'marshmallow'. The film ends on a Tuesday, and he says he's going to Detroit on Wednesday. Is he escaping to a better life, or just escaping?
Linnea Reese (Lily Tomlin)	The kindest person in *Nashville*. She adores her two deaf children and inexplicably sings (very poorly) in a Black gospel group and attends a Black church. She doesn't want to cheat on her husband, but she does want to sleep with Tom. She sleeps with Tom. Ultimately, she's the only woman impervious to his emotional abuse. In a film with too many characters for anyone to have a fully developed trajectory, she is a whole person with whom viewers have satisfyingly travelled by the end.

Character (Actor)	Description
Del Reese (Ned Beatty)	Husband of Linnea. Disconnected from his deaf children. Local political connection for Triplette. An exploiter at heart. You might hate him, but you might also pity him when he makes hard-boiled eggs with his belt hanging loose, as he wonders if his wife might be having an affair.
John Triplette (Michael Murphy)	Amoral, soulless political operative for Hal Phillip Walker. Contemptuous of 'country crapola' music but eager to use the 'local yokels' for political gain. Triplette reveals the worst in people.
Opal (Geraldine Chaplin)	Claims to be a journalist, but it's iffy. A satirical, unlikeable character who says outrageously foolish things. Beds Tom, but that's not hard to do.
Kenny Fraiser (David Hayward)	Appears to be a drifter, wandering through town with a violin case that has a poor caricature of himself taped to it. That, plus an uncomfortable phone conversation with his mother, seem to spell 'psycho!', a suspicion that is confirmed at the end of the film.
PFC Glenn Kelly (Scott Glenn)	Might be stalking Barbara Jean, yet he seems more thoughtful than obsessive. Always in military uniform, a red flag for countercultural and/or anti-Vietnam War viewers.
Albuquerque (Barbara Harris)	Running from her husband, seeking musical stardom, in increasingly distressed clothes, sleeping in cars, finding food where she can. Undeveloped, yet ultimately important to the film.
Star (Bert Remsen)	Husband to Albuquerque and determined to prevent her from becoming a singer. Calls her only by her old name, Winifred. Remains an undeveloped character.
Tricycle Man (Jeff Goldblum)	Rides throughout the film on a three-wheel motorcycle. Performs charming sleight of hand behind oversized glasses. Character remains undeveloped, but he pops up like a shiny penny throughout.
Tommy Brown (Timothy Brown)	Black country music singer, which makes him an odd man out, but remains undeveloped.
Norman (David Arkin)	Chauffeur to the Bill, Mary and Tom trio. Character remains undeveloped but used briefly in one scene to underscore Opal's callousness.

With this table of characters for reference, we are ready to dive into the film itself.

Day one: 'All right twirlers, let's twirl!'

Nashville begins with a strange preface, an alarming spinning image of what appears to be the soundtrack of the film being offered for sale, in the style of K-Tel, the marketer who hawked LPs on late-night TV in the 1970s. An announcer-carnival-barker type shouts out the names of all the actors and repeats the film's title, his voice layered over snippets of songs from the film, in an almost indecipherable audio mix. The brash opening is disconcerting on multiple fronts. Why is there a TV ad at the beginning of a movie? And wait, a title card has just informed viewers that the film is an ABC production. The network funded the picture under the mistaken assumption that money could be made on soundtrack record sales and a TV release. Is Altman making fun of that very idea to kick off his film, and, if so, isn't that a pretty big slap in the face for the money men upon whom

his very livelihood depends? An album was indeed released, designed in patriotic red, white and blue, but it never hit the country charts, though Carradine's Academy Award-winning 'I'm Easy' reached #72 on *Billboard*'s 'hot 100 singles' list for 1976.

At the same time that the vertigo-inducing, TV-like opener is loud and brash, however, it's also fun. Altman is embracing the crudeness of television. Conversely, many directors of the 1960s and 1970s rejected TV as garbage. Such contempt is the entire organising premise of Lumet's *Network* (1976) and is at the core of Wexler's *Medium Cool* (1969), the title itself a goofy twist on Marshall McLuhan's idea that television was a 'cool medium'. Altman embarked on a career in television in the late 1950s, but he was quickly bored by the imperative to shoot the same master shots and close-ups for every episode, and frustrated by being completely shut out of editing and casting decisions. Serial TV production was powered by a sausage factory mentality, which he fled for the more creative possibilities of feature-film production. But he wasn't snobbish about what the intelligentsia used to call 'the idiot box'. On the contrary, TV plays in the background in a number of his films, functioning as a sort of wallpaper of American life. For better or for worse, TV is just *there*, and it could even be used for good, as Altman found when he returned to television production later in his career. There was even a serious idea brewing to create a six- or eight-part TV miniseries version of *Nashville* that would reveal all kinds of character relationships and twists that had been shot but not included in the theatrical release.[33] The idea faltered once the movie did not live up to box-office expectations, but it is spoken about as a sure thing in numerous 1975 interviews.

Following *Nashville*'s crazy TV-style opening, we hear Hal Phillip Walker promote his flimsy political ideas from his sound truck as it drives through downtown, past mom-and-pop furniture stores and the Mini Adult Cinema. And then we get to the meat and potatoes of the opening, Haven Hamilton (Henry Gibson) singing 'We must be doing something right to last 200 years'. The next

written by
joan tewkesbury

two-plus hours reveal that this is not in fact the case. Americans have done almost everything wrong, as individuals and as a society. This scene in the recording studio sets the stage not only for the political undercurrents that will churn throughout the film but also the dominant aesthetic – the zooms in and out, the lack of standard shot/reverse shots and, of course, the overlapping dialogue.

Linnea Reese (Lily Tomlin) is in another room in the same recording studio, where she performs as the front woman for a Black gospel choir. She's joyous, her dancing ecstatic, as she sings 'Do you believe in Jesus?' in a high-pitched falsetto. Sueleen Gay, to whom we have not yet been introduced, is later presented as the only obviously 'bad' singer in the film, but no one comments on Linnea's strangely high-pitched performance. The reason perhaps is that she is so enraptured that all one perceives of her performance is joy: the voicing doesn't matter because the emotion is pure, arguably the film's only moment of true happiness. This is the best it's gonna get, and this is still the credit sequence! The moment is semi-public; the audience comprises just the other singers, technicians, Haven's son Bud (Dave Peel) and Opal (Geraldine Chaplin), the absurd BBC radio journalist. (Or so she claims.) Pure expressivity is more important than audience or spectacle here; in a film full of celebrities and would-be celebrities, Linnea sings with no interest in stardom or public appreciation. This establishes her as the humanist core of *Nashville*.

One fact that might elude a viewer some fifty years later is that Tomlin and Gibson were the film's two biggest stars. Both had appeared on the hit TV show *Laugh-In* (1968–73). Casting Gibson as a heavy was about the smartest twist since Sergio Leone cast Henry Fonda as the villain in *Once Upon a Time in the West* (1968). On *Laugh-In*, Gibson was known for holding a flower and reciting silly poems. He had taken the stage name 'Henry Gibson' as a joke, because when you said it aloud it sounded like 'Henrik Ibsen'. Haven Hamilton's big hit 'Keep a' Goin'', sung on Saturday night at the Grand Ole Opry, clearly evoked his *Laugh-In* persona; the lyrics, originally written by Georgia's first poet laureate in 1900, had earlier

Henry Gibson on NBC's hit TV show *Laugh-In* (1968-73) (Andrew Maclear/Hulton Archive/Getty Images)

Haven Hamilton was partly modelled on Nashville star Hank Snow
(David Redfern/Getty Images)

been recited by Gibson on a 1966 episode of *The Dick Van Dyke Show* (1961–6). Hamilton had initially been written for Robert Duvall, but when Altman realised he couldn't afford him, he turned to Gibson, who had had a menacing cameo in *The Long Goodbye*. The Gibson version of Haven Hamilton was partly modelled on Hank Snow, a Nashville character likewise known for his bejewelled pantsuits, diminutive stature and unconvincing toupee. Gibson himself commissioned Haven's toupee from a top Hollywood wig man who had worked for Fred Astaire and Burt Reynolds. He later recounted, 'I asked him to make a wig with an obvious flaw in it. It blew his mind. Like asking Matisse to do less than a masterpiece.'[34]

Tomlin was also brilliantly cast against type as Linnea – originally imagined as a part for Louise Fletcher, who had played a heavy in *Thieves Like Us*. On *Laugh-In*, Tomlin was known for her adenoidal telephone operator character Ernestine, her smartass little girl Edith Ann and her parodic yet realistic portrayal of housewife Judith Beasley. In a strange way, in *Nashville*, she's playing off this last persona, by being a different sort of housewife. Tewkesbury

Lily Tomlin developed a range of characters on *Laugh-In*, such as her adenoidal telephone operator Ernestine (Bettmann/Getty Images)

herself noted a strong identification with the character: 'Linnea was based on me and a lot of women I know in those kinds of dilemmas – women in their early thirties that have lived in a particular construct all their lives and suddenly say "there's something else outside."'[35] No one at the time would have expected Lily Tomlin to be the throbbing heart of *Nashville*, doing serious acting. And yet there she was, nailing it. Demonstrating the wild improbability of the whole thing, in the playful 1976 independent video *TVTV Looks at the Oscars*, Tomlin appeared as herself, an Oscar nominee for *Nashville*, in gown and diamond tiara, and also as a variation on Judith Beasley watching Lily Tomlin on TV at the Academy Award ceremony (and watching herself lose to Lee Grant for *Shampoo*, a film with too much sex in it, the Beasley-like viewer complains). That Gibson and Tomlin both play with and against the personae they had crafted on *Laugh-In* adds significantly to *Nashville*'s pathos as an unnerving sometimes-comedy.

The rest of Friday introduces the remaining characters, starting with the arrival and almost immediate collapse of Barbara Jean (Ronee Blakley) at the airport. Here, an oversized performance by enthusiastic baton twirlers seems to confirm the excess signalled by the K-Tel parody ad. The girls are in sequined leotards and plastic diamond tiaras, marching with American and Confederate flags. The energy is loud, manic even, as Haven Hamilton cries out, 'All right twirlers, let's twirl!' The notion that entertainers are more highly valued than politicians in America is confirmed by the fact that Walker campaign workers are also at the airport, but only drifting in the background or waving signs to try to get shown on TV. It is Barbara Jean who people care about. Asked by a campaign worker in the crowd if he will vote for Walker, the popular singer Tom (Keith Carradine) grunts that he

votes for no one, then turns to a man in uniform (ardent Barbara Jean fan PFC Kelly [Scott Glenn]) and brutally asks him if he's 'killed anybody this week?' Tom here embodies the film's cynicism: there's no point in voting; why bother after Vietnam and the re-election of Nixon? The moment also taps into viewers' prejudices, presuming that liberals will intuitively side with the longhair Tom against the soldier Kelly. The twist will later emerge that Tom is a womanising creep, whereas Kelly is a pretty nice guy.

Carradine had previously been in two Altman films, first as a pathetic but kindly kid who got himself shot dead in his long underwear in *McCabe and Mrs. Miller* and later as the also-slaughtered bank robber in *Thieves Like Us*. The *Nashville* audience familiar with these earlier roles was probably quite small compared to those who recognised TV stars Tomlin and Gibson, but for those who knew Carradine's earlier work with Altman, Tom's icy cruelty would have been even more shattering. Scott Glenn was also a relative unknown, and was also playing against type, if any *Nashville* viewers happened to recognise him from *Angels Hard as They Come*, a sleazy 1971 biker picture produced by Roger Corman and directed by Jonathan Demme. And just to throw in one more perplexing bit of esoteric context, Carradine and Glenn had appeared together, with Cristina Raines (Mary in *Nashville*) and Gary Busey (the original casting choice for Tom in *Nashville*), in *Hex*, a 1973 Western-supernatural-horror-biker film. Altman's casting decisions were spontaneous and instinctive, and he almost always got it right, but it's rather strange to realise that his masterpiece, epic film was cast with not only big stars of a TV show specialising in silly birth control jokes and countercultural mockery but also actors known for low-rent drive-in pictures.

Shortly after the airport scene, a highway traffic collision forces everyone to be stuck in one place, as the omniscient camera moves from car to car. This is a plot device that remained from Tewkesbury's original script, based on an experience she had while researching the film. The overlapping dialogue here is cacophonous, overwhelming a viewer trying to keep track of each character. This subsides after the traffic pile-up, though, as the importance of sound shifts in new directions, as pointed to in three scenes.

First, Linnea and Del (Ned Beatty) interact at home with their two deaf children, the twist being that it has up to now been difficult for hearing viewers to make sense of things, and now they are suddenly confronted with non-hearing people. Linnea doesn't need sound to communicate because she can sign, while Del flounders, having apparently never made an effort to learn American Sign Language. The pointed message has been conveyed: it was hard to follow this film when the dialogue was wildly fluctuating and the music was loud, but if you were *trying* to decipher meaning you were on the right track, like Linnea. The problem is not so much that people don't understand others, but, rather, that sometimes, like Del, they don't even attempt to understand. Interpersonal communication is not going to be easy for the characters in this film, and what makes it worse is that some of the characters could not care less about that crisis.

Second, as the family eats with their guest, political operative John Triplette, Tom calls Linnea on the phone to try to set up a sexual encounter. Now we are listening to a muted phone voice, as heard by Linnea. It's disconcerting, because that's not how films of the era (and earlier) conventionally represented phone calls – they

normally cut back and forth between locations, or used a split screen, or just provided audio for the person pictured on screen, but not for the speaker on the other end. It's awkward to experience it this way. Tom's muted voice sounds recorded because of its technical mediation. Tom and Linnea's conversation was not crafted in post-production. Rather, it was all recorded synchronously as the actors spoke to each other. From the aural perspective of the film's viewer-listener, it's as if Linnea's phone is being bugged, and we're eavesdropping. In other words, this is a private conversation that feels 'dirty' to Linnea because it is a sexual advance, and also feels 'dirty' to viewers because they are illicitly listening in. The existence of Nixon's White House taping system had been revealed in 1973, and his refusal to hand over the subpoenaed tapes was no small factor in his impeachment, underway as the film was shot in July and August 1974. There's no explicit Nixon reference in the Tom–Linnea exchange, but by the time of *Nashville*'s release in 1975 it's hard to imagine anyone would have felt neutral about a movie scene requiring the audience to listen in on a private phone conversation. A later scene in the film drives home the surveillance angle, when Tom once again calls to proposition Linnea, and she acts as if she doesn't know him, specifically because she is aware that her husband is listening in on another line in the house.

Third, Sueleen sings at an open mic event at a club, and it's just excruciatingly bad, an assault to the ear. One person immediately cries out, 'it's awful!' You'll never hear a worse singer in any film – or in real life, for that matter – and this is one element that points to *Nashville* as perhaps an anti-musical, just as *McCabe and Mrs. Miller* is an anti-Western. Singers are never terribly, terribly bad in musicals. Lina Lamont aside (and the whole damn point of *Singin' in the Rain* [1952] is that we must never hear her objectionable voice), it simply isn't done. Reviewers were cruel about Sueleen's lack of talent. Canby complained she 'can't even carry off a striptease without bungling', a callous comment on a scene of sexual violation, and Kael described her as a stupid, 'luscious bimbo', though also irresistible.[36] What such unkind commentators fail to notice is the very first time Sueleen sings in *Nashville*, at the airport diner where she works, in a fleeting, intimate moment with a stranger. This is one of many important blink-and-you'll-miss-it moments in the film. It stands out because Sueleen is genuinely happy, smiling and flirting and leaning in to sing her song 'I Never Get Enough' to just one person, the charming Tricycle Man (Jeff Goldblum). Her voice is not particularly good, but it registers as sweet and kind, specifically because this is a low-key, human interaction, wholly distinct from the public performances throughout the film by celebrities and would-be celebrities. To perform for a

crowd is most often an act of artifice, even if you are good. To perform for one person is genuine, the scene seems to indicate. This is a hopeful moment in a film often understood as cynical. Even here, the beauty of the fleeting moment is undercut by a cutaway to Del, who feels his first moment of lecherous desire for Sueleen.

Later that afternoon, Sueleen briefly performs solo in her bedroom, practising for the open mic show. Her rehearsal is disconcerting on several counts. When she performed at the diner, it was a genuinely private, albeit fleeting moment. In the privacy of her bedroom, however, she is awkward and stilted, imagining an audience before her. The painfulness is exponentially amplified by the stuffing of sweat socks into her bra. She's already wearing a cut-out pantsuit, and the homemade falsies add a pathetic dimension to the notion that sex appeal will boost her vocal performance, which she assumes will be exceptional, because she is certain that she is a terrific singer.

It seems clear that Sueleen's performance that night at the club cannot be understood simply as acting in any conventional sense. Gwen Welles, who plays Sueleen, is an exceptional actress, and yet when she sings in public we are painfully aware that what we are seeing is *real*, on the level of pornography or snuff movies, where the bodies are actually doing something that in other movies would be faked. Welles is a terrible singer, and she was actually *coached* to reach the level of proficiency she achieved in *Nashville*. The sheer atrocity of this singing voice makes people react unkindly in the film, but it offers the cringing viewer an opportunity to feel empathy. In a film of disconnection, and where sex in particular is used more for harm than intimacy, our feelings for Sueleen as she sings confirm that human connection is extraordinarily difficult but not impossible. The film is dark but not hopeless. As Altman himself once put it in an interview, he was not an optimist, but he hadn't given up: he called himself a 'hopeful cynic, a person who lives in the desert and hopes for rain'.[37]

By Friday night, as the day closes out, the film has signalled that even if the cacophonous overlapping dialogue of the earliest scenes has settled down, viewers will continue to be pushed to think of themselves as listeners in a way that is quite different from what they encounter in other films. Listening will never be neutral or taken for granted in *Nashville*.

Day two: 'Any one of you can grow up to be the president!'

Saturday opens with Tom kicking BBC reporter Opal out of his motel bed. 'Being dirty' is literalised, as Altman's low camera reveals her feet landing behind a sad pile-up of paté de foie garbage in the foreground. 'Casual sex' implies a rather easy-going encounter,

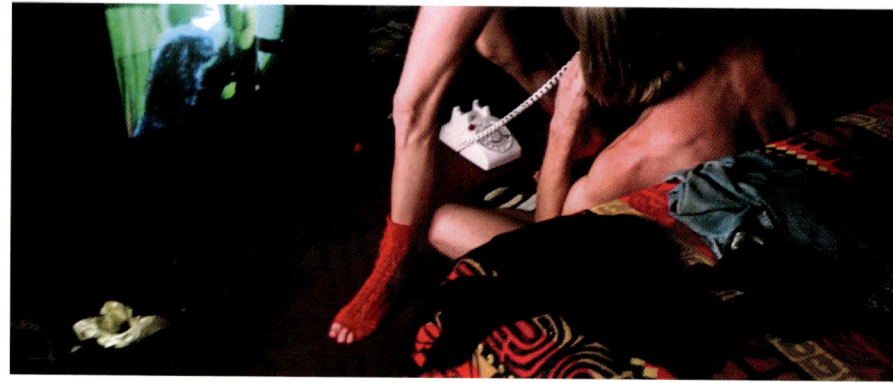

but for Tom, once the sex is done, there's no point in even attempting politeness. Besides, he's got his usual busy schedule to attend to. For starters, he needs to get out of bed himself, sit on the floor in his birthday suit and get back to courting Linnea over the telephone, while *Sesame Street* plays on the TV in the background. He proceeds to this work, while Opal wanders off in her holey socks, improvising nonsense commentary on her tape recorder. As she steps over Tom to reach her underpants, the camera shows de-eroticised naked limbs rather than faces. The two may have copulated the night before, but they could not possibly have less interest in one another in the morning.

By midday, everyone shows up at Haven's house for a cookout, and Elliott Gould, then one of America's most popular actors, makes a cameo appearance that is disconcertingly low-key.[38] *Nashville* is full of people who want to be celebrities, but here's a real star, and he's just incredibly cool and out of their league. The actor appears, in reality, simply because he was passing through town while promoting Altman's 1974 release *California Split*; viewed that way, the cameo seems like a cheap throwaway on Altman's part. On the other hand, in its portrait of America, *Nashville* includes characters who are famous or seeking celebrity, and one recurring idea of the film is not a fierce criticism but more like a statement, with little judgement:

'America is a place where many people want to be famous.' Fame might be a hollow aspiration, but if you are sufficiently cynical, that's not really a pressing problem. As per the song Tom sang on a reel-to-reel player in the motel, as he smoked in bed beside Opal, 'You may say that I ain't free, but it don't worry me.'

The closest thing to a real criticism of celebrity in the film lies in the character of Haven, a power-hungry egomaniac. Being famous is an important part of his power, and he wants his son Bud, a recent Harvard law school graduate who he holds up like a trophy, to reflect well on him. Tewkesbury drew original inspiration for Bud from a college friend, future sitcom star John Ritter, who was forever in the shadow of his superstar musician dad Tex Ritter, remembered best by cinephiles today as the singer of the *High Noon* (1952) anthem. Like John, Bud aspired to get into showbiz, but his father wanted him to be a lawyer. Unlike Bud's dad Haven, John's dad Tex did not pretend a disinterest in politics, having supported Goldwater and Reagan. He even presented a tribute album to Nixon in the White House entitled *Thank You, Mr. President*.

Country music star Tex Ritter presents the *Thank You, Mr. President* LP to Nixon in December 1973 (Bettmann/Getty Images)

When Triplette asks Haven to sing with Barbara Jean at a rally for Hal Phillip Walker, he and his companion Lady Pearl insist that they aren't political. It's a telling counterpoint to Tom's earlier cynicism at the airport. Hippies and longhairs like Tom don't vote because they are angry or disaffected; big stars don't vote (or say who they vote for) because taking a stand might alienate some of their fans, but they do this under the guise of neutrality. And yet when Triplette indicates Walker could help Haven be elected governor, Haven takes the bait without a second thought. Supporting a candidate is for suckers, unless you get something in return. To *believe* in political ideals is beyond the ken of any character in this film. That's Altman's vision of where America is after the 1960s, after Vietnam and after Nixon. It's worth adding that the idea of a big Nashville country music star feigning disinterest in politics was perhaps far-fetched, given that Nashville was for the most part a right-wing town. Triplette points to this on Friday during the traffic jam when he tells Del, 'I think people down here feel that movie stars are eccentric, crazy, communists … a lot of them are.'

The film's next key scene is at the Grand Ole Opry, where Connie White (Karen Black) substitutes for the re-hospitalised Barbara Jean, and Haven offers up a thin song about breaking up with his mistress: 'For the sake of the children, we must say goodbye.'

He's short and stiff, in a sparkling white pantsuit with star appliqués. Tommy Brown (Timothy Brown) sings an innocuous tune about bluebirds, and as he exits Haven says under his breath, 'you're lucky to be alive,' apparently indicating that the crowd could have torn him to bits just for being a Black country singer. The scene is designed to build character more than to progress any kind of narrative or to entertain with musical numbers, although there are several of them. Connie White crouches down in her junior prom dress to sign autographs and pet some moppets on the head, telling them they should 'study real hard because just remember, any one of you can grow up to be the president!' That's the American way. One of them takes a photo of Connie as she coos to them, confirming her celebrity status. This is exactly as she likes it. Working Nashville musicians accompany all the songs, and the regular Grand Ole Opry announcers do their promos for Goo Goo Clusters and King Leo Stick Candy, a reminder to those in the know that the Grand Ole Opry provides a stage show for a small audience but also, simultaneously, a sponsored radio show for a much wider Southern audience of radio listeners.

Meanwhile, back at the hospital, Barnett (Allan Garfield) is glued to the radio to hear Connie White perform in his wife's place. Barbara Jean is aggravated by hearing her rival, and an argument quickly escalates as Barnett says, 'Don't tell me how to promote.

Don't tell me how to run your life. I've been doing pretty good with it.' The scene could end there, because once you've cruelly told your wife not to tell you how to run her life, it's clear that she is something of a non-person to you, and there is nowhere to go but down. Indeed, the exchange spirals, and within moments Barbara Jean is herself on the floor, having cast her get-well flowers everywhere and finally melted down like a Goo Goo Cluster on asphalt. 'Are you THROUGH … are you going nutsy on me?' Barnett demands, two interrogatives that are actually declaratives: she is through, and she is going nutsy. In fact, she has never stopped going nutsy. 'Why do you make me raise my voice to you?' Barnett asks, the textbook words of an abusive husband. The partly submerged patriarchal hostility of Altman's earlier *Countdown* is all here on the surface. Finally, the scene closes out as Barnett coerces a dutiful 'bye-bye' from his wife and leaves her shuddering in bed, alone. Barbara Jean is a star on stage, yet at the bottom of the pecking order when her husband is in the picture. She has talent and a career. She is a figure relentlessly in the public eye. And yet her only path forward is to retreat hysterically within, expressing herself via nervous collapse. Barnett forces Barbara Jean to say goodbye to him, as one would a small child, and then departs for the King of the Road club to thank Connie, offering her a corsage that she flatly refuses.

There's a pecking order here, and the only person Barnett can dominate is his wife. And so he does. Being a regional superstar offers protection to Connie, who has the luxury of not only rejecting Barnett's flowers but also not recognising the much bigger star Julie Christie (no doubt a communist, as per Triplette's earlier quip) when she inexplicably stops by the table at the King of the Road. White's a big fish in a small pond, and Christie doesn't care either way, like Elliott Gould at Haven's place. Prompted by Triplette, Del recognises Christie as a big star, but Christie is as cool as a cucumber, and Connie assumes it's all a joke, since she looks like some kind of hippy: 'She can't even comb her hair!' Up on the stage at the King of the Road, the emcee announces that there's a big star in the audience, and Haven puffs himself up like a bird and starts to rise, assuming he will be invited to perform, but instead it is Connie who is invited. Yet just moments earlier he was king at the Opry. How can fame be so precarious? How can some women be more powerful than men, and other women never achieve a baseline sense of their own agency? How can the woman who is at the very top of the Nashville singing scene, Barbara Jean, exert no power or authority whatsoever? It seems that everyone wants to be Barbara Jean ... except for Barbara Jean. The sequence from the hospital to the King of the Road is a sad, concise study of the tyranny of hierarchies.

The day finally circles back to where it began, in Tom's unkempt motel room, where he is asleep in bed next to Mary. She desperately repeats 'I love you', but the postcoital Tom is down for the count. Conservative American viewers who rejected the New Hollywood films often decried their representation of sex outside marriage, but what's particularly jarring in *Nashville* by the end of Saturday is its portrait not of hot bedroom scenes but of cold bedroom scenes.

Day three: 'I'm a registered Democrat!'

It's Sunday. This is the shortest day in the film; not much seems to happen. Everyone (almost) goes to church. The devout Kennedy follower Lady Pearl is of course a Catholic and so attends mass. Sueleen, too, attends mass, striking because she (like Lady Pearl) wears a large kerchief on her head, an old-school gesture a decade after the modernising shifts brought by Vatican II. On Friday we saw Sueleen's bedroom, which was partly decorated with religious iconography, her dresser cluttered with a lava lamp, hairdryer, Virgin Mary statues, a sad little fishbowl and holy cards. She's a true believer. But it's inherently jarring to see someone who has worn immodest pantsuits with cut-outs and zippers, and who has stuffed her bra with sweat socks, appear in church in an extremely conventional and devout guise. That said, her bedroom did have

a painting of a saint (perhaps the Virgin Mary) on the wall, with a gorgeous image of herself below it, posed like a silent movie star in an old-fashioned photograph, with a gauzy wrap around her shoulders. An angel she is, this tone-deaf, simple soul. Sueleen even attends a mass where Latin is still sung.

Cut next to a large Protestant church choir. If you haven't thought much about religion in the South, the two church scenes might look pretty similar, but Protestants sing in English, not Latin. In the 1970s, Catholics were denigrated as 'papists' by evangelicals, and a surge in liberal Catholicism in the 1960s and 1970s only increased anti-Catholic feelings on the Right. It's unclear how plugged into this Altman was, but Lady Pearl (as improvised by Barbara Baxley) understood: in a drunken monologue about JFK at the King of the Road the night before, she had said, 'the problem we got here is anti-Catholicism. These dumbheads around here, they're all Baptists and whatever.' It's fair to say that if Nashville's predominantly white and evangelical movie audience rejected the film mostly for its liberalism and poor-quality music, featuring two Catholic characters worshipping did nothing to warm them up to the picture. Haven, of course, is a God-fearing Protestant, and he even sings in his church's choir; one instinctively feels that he's putting on an act, showing off that he can sing like an ordinary, non-famous person. Del's there, too,

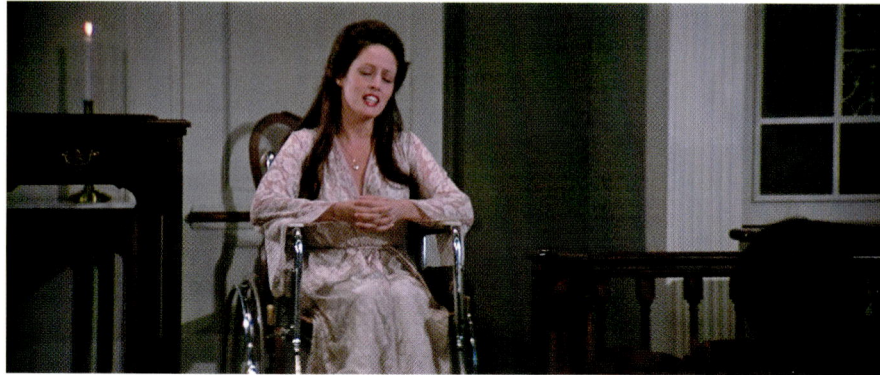

with the kids, but not his wife. Next up is another Protestant church, this one Black. Linnea sings in the choir, which is puzzling, but also confirms that her earlier scene at the recording studio was not a fluke. Meanwhile, in a small and spare hospital chapel, Barbara Jean sings the classic hymn 'In the Garden' from her wheelchair, wearing a graceful dressing gown of lace, a mere mortal before a small audience of fellow supplicants. It's the first time we've heard her sing, and she is notably without a microphone and appears truly at ease for this private performance. Another woman sits in a wheelchair in the aisle. No one sings along as at the other churches. Some are moved, others wrapped up in their own thoughts. If you are at a hospital chapel on a Sunday morning, in a Southern town where everyone goes to *their own* church every Sunday, something out of the ordinary or urgent is happening. A relative may be dying.

From this gentle scene, a sudden cut to Opal wandering about a scrapyard improvising an inane monologue into her portable tape recorder about decaying auto corpses is absurd and jarring. 'I'm reminded of an elephant's secret burial ground!' she exclaims, as church bells gently ring. 'Oh cars, are you trying to tell me something?!' Continuing with this now wholly secular Sunday afternoon, Altman cuts to the racetrack, where Haven almost gets in trouble for offering Tommy Brown a piece of *watermelon* (get it, he's Black), which an appalled Opal switches out for iceberg lettuce. We've very quickly departed the reverential for the mundane cruelties of daily life.

Back in their hotel room, Bill (Allan Nicholls) and Mary argue, the chaos of the room expressing their disdain for each other, with piles of clothing, empty beer bottles and old room-service platters scattered about. As the shouting accelerates, Mary adds to the mess by dumping out a dresser drawer, while on the TV a happy couple discovers the joy of cooking with Reynolds Wrap, a perfect commentary on the discrepancy between mass media fantasies and the cold, hard reality of human relationships. Tewkesbury said about Bill and Mary:

I made a breach in their marriage, and the thing that I wanted to be the most violent, other than the violent act [of Barbara Jean's assassination] at the end, was the violence that was going down between them – the controlled violence that we live with every day. It's the most volatile kind, and it's awful, 'cause they keep biting their tongues and being nice, while deep down they hate each other.[39]

The dispute is interrupted by the arrival of Triplette, who has come to ask if they would perform for his man, the Replacement Party candidate, at a big upcoming rally. He woos Bill by saying, 'I just want to tell you a little bit about what we're trying to do … I know you're astute politically, and I'm certainly not here to sell you a bill of goods.' The line is meant to deceive: he surely does not think Bill and Mary are very bright, and he is there precisely to sell them a bill of goods, a point driven home when Bill asks if the rally will be shown on network TV, and Triplette replies, 'No, it's really better than network, it's going to be syndicated.' Now, a number of TV shows have been very successful in first-run syndication (much of the *Star Trek* franchise, for example), but at the same time, syndication, whereby programmes are sold piecemeal on a station-by-station basis, was certainly viewed in 1975 as the most low-rent sort of distribution,

regardless of how profitable it may have been. A political rally for a candidate of any reputation would have been aired on network, and to indicate otherwise is the most duplicitous sort of used-car salesman manipulation. That's pure Triplette. Mary displays her contempt for him, as she smears cold cream on her face, and claims that she and Bill cannot perform for Walker at the Parthenon because they are 'registered Democrats'. On the one hand, she's just mad at Bill and being contrary. On the other hand, one is reminded of Haven the previous day. Mary doesn't want to support the Replacement Party candidate, but not because of her genuine political beliefs. As Bill

points out, they are only registered Democrats because her father is a registered Democrat. No one in this film expresses political beliefs one could take seriously as 'genuine'. Triplette even says, with a laugh, 'I'm a registered Democrat!' to convince Bill and Mary to play at the Parthenon, but his words are obviously meaningless.

Finally, Tom, still in his 'grand motel' room, asks Norman the chauffeur (David Arkin) if he can get him some uppers. Mary, who was in bed with him the night before, had left earlier to return to Bill. She's written 'I love you' in lipstick on Tom's mirror, right above his Right Guard and an empty carafe of Paul Masson, the saddest of wines. Tom doesn't see the note, and if he did, it's hard to imagine a more energetic response than 'I wonder which chick wrote that?'

Day four: 'I'm happy I met you'

Given the kaleidoscopic approach to characters and their stories, a viewer (especially an overwhelmed new viewer) might feel that *Nashville* is a film without a climax, with the exception of the violent act that occurs on Tuesday. But that act is more like pulling the emergency brake on a train than it is a culmination of characterisation and story-building. The key emotional climaxes of *Nashville* occur on Monday. You need everything before and after to make sense of day four, to understand why it all matters, but if you extracted this day alone, you'd have the soul of the film. *Nashville* is cynical and cruel at times. If voting is pointless, human emotional connection is elusive and even sex doesn't seem like any fun, what is left? There's humour, and the film has some of that, suggesting that while absurdity is not a cure, it will help you keep your head above water. And there's also singing, which when it works provides the sort of ineffable emotional release offered by more conventional musicals. Three pivotal Monday scenes are notable for the empathic, erotic and ethical demands they make upon the viewer, affirming that we should care about human connection and disconnection.

In the first of these three key scenes, Barbara Jean sings several songs at an outdoor venue at Opryland, and it's beautiful. Next, she spirals into stories about her childhood and chickens and her grandmother's false teeth. It's the part of the performance where 'banter' would usually be normal; we've seen this chatty convention many times during live performances, as earlier when Connie White did her phoney Grand Ole Opry schtick. But Barbara Jean doesn't have the emotional resources to conjure up this sort of fake intimacy with her audience, and so she conjures instead real intimacy with her unhinged storytelling. It starts off fairly normally, but soon she is saying that she can sing like a Munchkin and is fond of *The Wizard of Oz*, and then she spirals off the deep end with a full-throated imitation of a clucking chicken. She is finally escorted from the stage by Barnett. The empathic core of the film lies in this scene. A reverse shot of the audience reveals that PFC Kelly and Kenny (David Hayward) are worried, Opal is disgusted and the rest of the audience is disappointed not to hear a full show. As hostile fans boo and throw things at the stage, Barnett promises that Barbara Jean will appear the next day at the Parthenon, a promise made in a moment of spite, with no thought regarding whether his wife can mentally survive another public performance. The audience has been cruel and thoughtless, but so has Barnett. He has lived up to our low expectations following the hospital scene, but strangely, one expects more from the worshipful crowd of strangers. Barbara Jean's monologue, written by Ronee

Blakley herself, conveys her raw, naked vulnerability; she is a trapped woman with no hope of self-preservation. She closes out her childhood story by sputtering, 'Ever since then I've been working, I don't … I think ever since then I've been working, and doing my, supporting myself …', her words trailing off. She's exhausted from supporting herself. It's just a little slip but underscores the fact that while Barnett is running her life, as he has imperiously declared, she's the one actually doing the work.

Also on this day, Tom advances his seduction, calling Linnea to invite her to the Exit/In, a club where he's singing. The phone call is as jarring as their last, but this time, we only overhear Tom speak. Linnea cannot find words, her jaw slightly slackens, her breathing accelerates and she looks directly at the camera as it zooms in on her face. It's a hard thing to pull off in a dramatic scene, that stare at the camera. She's breathing too much, and yet I always catch myself not breathing during this scene. She hasn't decided yet what to do. Similarly at the Exit/In later, the camera zooms in and technically she looks right at it, but she almost seems to be looking past the lens, her expression aching with desire. Now she has decided. The erotic core of the film lies in this scene, when Tom sings 'I'm Easy', which he dedicates to 'someone special who just might be here tonight'. Such a clever bastard. His vague dedication ensures that multiple

women in the audience will imagine the song is directed to them. Tom will get lucky for sure, even if Linnea doesn't fall for his line. This is a key moment not only in terms of revealing character but also because the film is, atypically, in dialogue with the conventions of the musical genre. In musicals, romantic songs are often used to bring a couple closer together. In some cases, the couple is not in love at the beginning of the song, but their feelings have advanced to the next level by the end. The 'I'm Easy' scene is a different version of this, celebrating sex but not love, and casting a promiscuously wide net, undermining the whole premise of monogamous romantic love that drives most musicals.

Linnea's face, filled with longing, confirms that she, too, is easy. Linnea falls into the net, and into bed with Tom, following which he asks her how to sign 'I love you'. She shows him, but adds that an alternative is 'I'm happy I met you', as if to cover herself. She's said 'I love you' with her hands but wants to make clear that this is not how she feels. They are not in love, but the scene conveys intimacy and fleeting human connection. Meanwhile, Tom has also spoken the three special words with his hands. Does he mean it? Certainly not, but it's shocking that he asked her how to say it. At the very least, he feels *something* for this woman, and he is hurt when she leaves to get home before her husband, offering Tom a perfunctory kiss and

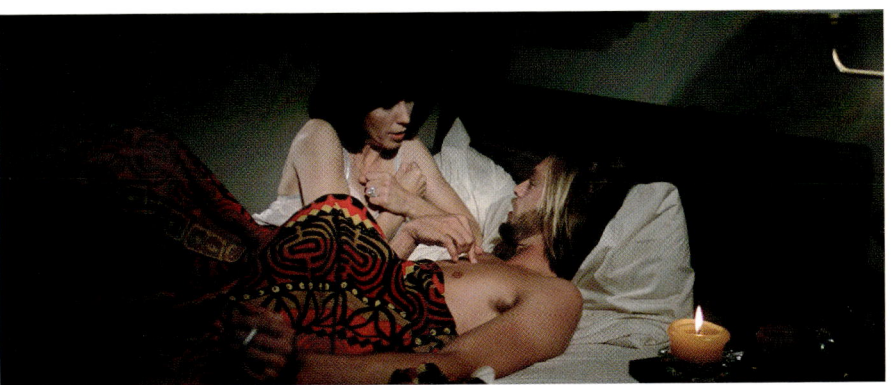

stuffing her panties in her purse on the way out. It turns out that there is a woman who can use Tom for sex instead of the reverse, a rather radical gender switch for a 1975 film. Linnea's quick exit is mediated by the mirror. She signs 'see you later' on her way out the door. Communication is thus doubly distanced, via hand gestures and reflection. Notably, Tewkesbury had been struggling to find a way for Linnea to exit this scene with dignity, and originally Tom was to have thrown Linnea's underpants at her as she made her way out. Tomlin nixed that. Further, she was to have been nude in the scene but decided against it, which for her very specifically evoked the 'bad women movies' she had viewed as a teenager. These films featured 'the only interesting women in the movies during that time, the only ones who had any independence or autonomy. In the fifties, they always wore a full slip. My reference was Lana Turner in *The Flame and the Flesh* [1954].'[40] This illustrates so clearly how improvisation impacted the film, at times making the gender politics so much more progressive and interesting than they might have been if actors had simply obeyed a script.

The ethical core of the film is the scene of Sueleen's forced striptease. Triplette and Del have staged a stag party as a Walker fundraiser, and Sueleen's the main attraction, but she's been told that she's there to sing. She sees it as the opportunity of a lifetime, at last

a real gig! As the crowd jeers and rejects her, she cannot understand why. Presuming that the stripping will start at any moment, Del and Budd are delighted by Sueleen's terrible singing. Ever the Machiavellian, only Triplette has figured out that something is awry. She finally tries to retreat from the venue, but Triplette and Del tell her she has to strip. Triplette needs campaign donations, and he will say or do anything to make that happen. To that end, he tells Suleen that if she strips, she can appear with Barbara Jean at the Parthenon rally the next day. Trapped, she caves in. The band strikes up a tinny burlesque tune as she peels off her clothes, starting with the socks

she's stuffed in her bra. Tewkesbury later said that this was one scene in the film that was performed exactly as written, except for the sweat socks,[41] a brilliant, de-eroticising improvisatory move on Welles's part. Sueleen is stiff, her face desperately unhappy, as she mechanically circles the room, aware that everyone is supposed to see her. Aside from the circling, she violates all the conventions of stripping: the slow removal, the tease, the pretence of seduction. Her dress even gets caught on her heels. The men hoot and holler with satisfaction, choosing not to register her performance as obviously lacking in eroticism. These men are worse than Tom, who goes beyond seeking consent: he wants women not just to say yes but to beg him for sex. Thus is the monstrosity of sexual exploitation itself laid bare by the forced striptease. These men are so engorged with rapacious desire that they will boo very poor-quality singing but cheer very poor-quality stripping. Who cares, as long as they get to see the goods? Sueleen could be a corpse hung up on marionette strings, and they'd still be aroused.

This level of sexual cruelty was still relatively new for American audiences. The industry's internal censor, the Production Code Administration, had managed Hollywood films from 1934 on, but a number of court decisions, in addition to industrial changes, the influx of adult-oriented foreign films, and shifting societal attitudes

about the representation of sex and violence, had all contributed
to the collapse of that self-censoring system by the late 1960s. The
door was open for more sophisticated art films, but also for more
ruthlessly cruel films – or at least, films that included scenes of cruelty.
Post-Code productions are packed with women who enjoy stripping,
prostitution and even rape. Consider the 'comic' scene in *Butch
Cassidy and the Sundance Kid* (1969), where the punchline is that
Sundance seems about to rape a woman, but the twist is that she's
already his lover. Consider, too, the 'seduction' scene in *Three Days
of the Condor*, when the protagonist berates his female hostage (yes,
hostage) into sleeping with him, and *she* ends up apologising to *him*
in the morning. Sueleen's striptease tells us that this is all complete
bullshit. In this way, her scene recalls the crucial moment in Alan J.
Pakula's *Klute* (1971), when Bree, a prostitute played by Jane Fonda,
gives all the indications of enjoying her work, and then mid-thrust
takes a very pointed look at her watch, undercutting every 'happy
hooker' type of scene you've ever seen in a movie.

Monday has held together and fallen apart, all based on song.
Barbara Jean has both succeeded and failed to sing on this day.
Tom has sung a woman right into bed. Sueleen has epically failed
to sing. For three days the film has suggested that maybe we should
care about people or maybe it's pointless, but now, at last, *Nashville*
confirms that people (especially male people) are at base mostly
terrible, but we shouldn't give up. If we can root for Linnea, who
seems to be in an unfulfilling marriage but has made a sexual choice
that matters because it is *her* choice, if we can shudder for Sueleen,
who deserves our respect regardless of her intelligence or skills, and
if we can understand why Barbara Jean, the biggest 'success' in the
film, is nonetheless emotionally shattered, then we have responded
with openness. As per the song that recurs throughout *Nashville* and
famously ends the film, you might not care about the economy or
tax relief or the price of bread or even the inevitability of death
('life may be a one-way street'), but if you are still capable of
sometimes worrying about other humans, well, that's something.

Day five: 'This isn't Dallas. It's Nashville'

The film's closing act takes place at the Parthenon, a to-scale duplicate of the original Greek edifice. Nashville's version was first built of wood and plaster and brick in 1897. Having crumbled away twenty years later, this duplicate was rebuilt in concrete. Tuesday's setting is, in other words, the copy of a copy, a rather perfect place to host a political rally for a faceless populist political candidate with few discernible policies. The point is driven home by the opening images at the rally. First, a transitional night-time shot of a blimp with an electric news crawl promoting Walker dissolves to a daytime shot of a TV set on a picnic table at the Parthenon. Who brings a twenty-pound 'portable' TV to a picnic? All we know is that it's a Walker supporter, because there's a bumper sticker on the side of the set. The image shows ABC newsman Howard K. Smith delivering an odd but somewhat informative commentary on Walker. The 'commentary' will probably not resonate strongly as a TV news subgenre for a viewer who grew up after the network era, because opinion, especially on cable, is much of what TV 'news' has become. But in 1975, the news strived for neutrality, and when a point of view was delivered it appeared at the end of a broadcast and was explicitly labelled as such.

Howard K. Smith had been at ABC since falling out with CBS in the wake of his 1961 documentary *Who Speaks for Birmingham?*[42]

Smith had witnessed the savage beating of the Freedom Riders at Birmingham's Trailways Bus Station, when Eugene 'Bull' Connor had allowed thugs a fifteen-minute free-for-all without police interference. Smith reported on that candidly, and then the local CBS station dropped its CBS affiliation, and the City of Birmingham sued the network for $1.5 million. Smith found himself in a 'you-can't-fire-me-I-quit' situation and left for ABC. ABC was considered the underdog network, and it was a demotion for Smith, but it did make him a big fish in a small pond. Thereafter, he cameoed as himself in several liberal movies, such as *The Best Man* (1964), an earnest anti-Goldwater film scripted by Gore Vidal, and *The Candidate* (1972), a Robert Redford film about the ethics of political campaigns.

Smith was a perfect match for *Nashville*. Like Altman, he was an independent thinker who irked management. When Altman invited him to appear as himself commenting on Walker, he told him to write his own material. The result is as strange as Walker himself:

Little more than a year ago, a man named Hal Phillip Walker excited a group of college students with some questions: Have you stood on a high and windy hill and heard the acorns drop and roll? Have you walked in the valley beside the brook, walked alone and remembered? Does Christmas smell like oranges to you? In a commencement speech such questions were fitting, perhaps, but hardly the material with which to launch a presidential campaign ... Hal Phillip Walker is, in a way, a mystery man. Out of nowhere, with a handful of students and scarcely any pros, he's managed to win three presidential primaries and is given a fighting chance to take a fourth, Tennessee. A win in that state would take on added significance, for only once in the last fifty years has Tennessee failed to vote for the winning presidential candidate ... Wherever he may be going, it seems sure that Hal Phillip Walker is not going away, for there is genuine appeal, and it must be related to the raw courage of this man – running for president, willing to battle vast oil companies, eliminate subsidies to farmers, tax churches, abolish the electoral college, change the national anthem and remove lawyers from government, especially from Congress. At this point it would be wise to say most of us don't know the answer to Hal Phillip Walker, but to answer one of his questions, as a matter of fact, Christmas *has* always smelled like oranges to me.

Walker's voice and his sound truck have been meandering in and out of the film, an important element not in the original Tewkesbury script and added to provide a more explicitly political slant, and yet it is only in this moment that we actually learn something about his story and why Tennessee is valuable to his campaign.[43] This is why the rally is important.

All of the film's characters are assembled on stage or watching from the audience, except for Connie White, who of course never appears in the same venue as her rival Barbara Jean. After a few beautiful songs, Barbara Jean is shot down by Kenny. It's inexplicable, but is it? Kenny has been brooding and wandering around for days with a violin case; there's a gun inside it, of course, like he's some kind of gangster manqué. Haven is shot in the arm, and his toupee flies off. The supremely vain man does not notice. Instead, stunned, he rejects offers of assistance and tells the others to take care of Barbara Jean instead. As Tom, Del, Barnett and the others instinctively come together to carry Barbara Jean off stage to an ambulance, Haven takes the microphone and says, 'Y'all take it easy now. This isn't Dallas. It's Nashville,' a reference to the 1963 Kennedy assassination. He then calls for someone to sing. The show must go on.

Of course, Nashville *is* Dallas if we take the violence there not as an aberration but as a wholly American occurrence. Dallas revealed America's identity as a country of assassins and extremists, and the violent acts of such men increasingly appeared live or almost-live on TV throughout the 1960s and 1970s. The brutal 1965 attack on the Selma-to-Montgomery marchers on the Edmund Pettus Bridge was filmed and shortly thereafter shown on network TV. The Detroit uprising in July 1967 was covered live, as the city burned for a week, and tanks and National Guardsmen filled the streets. The JFK assassination was captured live only on radio, but Jack Ruby

In July 1967, Detroit appeared as a war zone on the evening news (Smith Archive/Alamy); in August 1968, Chicago was transformed into an armed camp (Bettmann/Getty Images)

President Johnson's team watched King's assassination coverage on triple TVs as LBJ read ticker tape in the background (Everett Collection/Alamy)

murdered Lee Harvey Oswald as the nation watched on their sets. Bobby Kennedy was shot in June 1968 in Los Angeles, a tragedy covered live, though the shots were fired just beyong the camera's eye. A few months later, the police brutalised demonstrators in the streets of Chicago, as they chanted 'the whole world is watching'. National Guardsmen, police and Secret Service agents outnumbered Democratic National Convention protestors two to one.[44] Martin Luther King was felled the same year in Memphis, though cameras missed the moment of impact. Arthur Bremer shot and paralysed would-be Democratic presidential nominee George Wallace in Laurel, Maryland, in 1972. The assassination attempt was captured by an AP cameraman right in the thick of the action. On the *CBS Evening News*, Walter Cronkite reported RFK's widow Ethel's bedside visit – a shocking and poignant meeting of political opposites. In mid-July 1975, TV news reporter Christine Chubbuck of Sarasota, Florida, shot herself in the head during a live broadcast – not an assassination, but another horrific instance of televised gun violence. Understood in

Walter Cronkite reported the Wallace story, at a moment when
assassinations still disturbed but no longer surprised Americans
(CBS Photo Archive/Getty Images)

this wider, mediated American political context, the fictional Barbara
Jean's assassination during the filming of a political rally was jolting,
but only *surprising* because she was not Walker.

At any historical moment one could point to multiple instances
of American carnage, and this has only intensified with the rise of
mass shooting events in the twenty-first century, but it's notable
that it was exactly this context that framed the filming of *Nashville*,
weighing heavily on the actors as they improvised their performances.
Years later Henry Gibson aptly summarised the mood:

The tension was so thick ... The atmosphere in the country was totally focused on Watergate. Haldeman was indicted the day before we started the shooting. Earl Warren died. The focus was on the Supreme Court. Plus, there was tremendous violence. I think on the day of July fifth they indicted the man who stormed into a church and assassinated Martin Luther King's mother [on 30 July] ... This is four days before the picture begins. The progression was inescapable.

Gibson then recounts some of the brutal details of the Chubbuck suicide, an incident long forgotten that obviously made quite an impact at the time.[45] This is all the backstory one needs to understand why Haven Hamilton would desperately blurt out 'This isn't Dallas. It's Nashville.' He can't possibly believe what he's saying. His own spilled blood offers counter-evidence.

Like Hal Phillip Walker, *Nashville* doesn't take strong and coherent political positions, but it does convey a trenchant critique of soon to be post-Nixon America as a country in shambles – because of violence, because of racial conflict, because of human callousness and rampant lone gunmen. It's not always clear how the US has become this way, but perhaps it's by 'lasting' two hundred years without actually doing 'something right', or at least not enough right. The assassination of Barbara Jean might be understood as a cold

and cynical way to end the film. How sad to kill off this lovely and fractured woman – and even to film it for the TV syndication market. Someone once asked Altman why not shoot Walker instead, which would have been logical. He saw the question as barbaric, implying as it did that Barbara Jean just wasn't important enough to be murdered, but that the cold-blooded assassination of a candidate for political office would have been more palatable to viewers.

As horrific as the violence is, the finale also offers up some hopefulness. As Walker's limo speeds away (he's a populist who runs away with his tail between his legs when 'the people' are in trouble), Haven has for the first time shown himself as other-centred. Likewise, Tom has instinctively helped the team carry Barbara Jean's bleeding body. In a strange way, the ending mirrors the finale of *McCabe and Mrs. Miller*, when the town's church catches fire, and the raggedy townspeople, previously focused on boozing and gambling and fornicating, suddenly for the first time organically cohere as a community, passing buckets of water in a human chain, as if they cared about a house of worship. They don't exactly; the boozing and whoring (or being whored) will recommence the next day. Haven and Tom and the others spring into action when Barbara Jean is shot, but they will likewise revert to type. People are unlikely to change. After all, Linnea's default setting is the opposite of Tom's and Haven's; she is kind and true. She breaks from type by cheating with Tom, but by the next day she's back with her choir at the Parthenon, and also with Del, which may or may not be the best choice for her. The film has little faith that people can change, but it does have faith that sometimes people make good choices or simply experience transcendent moments – even seconds – of empathy. These flickering moments can help us 'keep a' goin''.

In any case, it is Albuquerque, wandering onto the stage as she has wandered throughout the entire picture, who takes the microphone, responding to Haven's plea, 'OK, everybody sing. Come on, somebody sing!' This day ultimately belongs to her. For most of *Nashville*, Albuquerque functions as disconcerting comic relief.

The recurring shtick has been that she wants to be a big singing star, but her husband is violently opposed to it – Altman-does-*I-Love-Lucy*. She has renamed herself Albuquerque, but her husband still calls her Winifred, a parallel to L.A. Joan, who used to be Martha but has taken a new name in order to recreate herself. Albuquerque first appears during the highway pile-up on Friday, sitting in a pickup truck and mumbling to her husband, Star (Bert Remsen), about how someone made a million dollars on a fly swatter with a red dot on the middle of it. She adds that differences between fly swatters have something to do with the Industrial Revolution. It seems like pure nonsense. She runs away from Star early on and is quickly reduced to sleeping in abandoned cars and rummaging for food. As the film progresses, she becomes more and more dishevelled, her stockings torn, the straps of her high heels hanging loose. Her first public performance is on Sunday at the racetrack, where she sings on a raised platform as cars whizz by. She makes broad gestures, pantomiming her feelings. Her song, in fact, is entitled

'With Gestures'. The cars are loud, and we can't hear a thing, as she flounces her arms up and down like a bird. It does seem that the scene is meant to be at her expense, a cruel gesture on Altman's part. It's not a moment seeking our empathy, unlike Sueleen's debut song at the open mic night and her later striptease. At the racetrack on Sunday, Albuquerque seems like the goofy version of Sueleen, an attractive woman, all looks but no talent. Of course this is not true, as is revealed during Albuquerque's climactic public performance following the assassination of Barbara Jean.

It turns out she is not the comic flipside of Sueleen after all. In fact, she's possibly the best singer in the film. She has previously seemed flighty and childish. And yet given a chance to express herself, she is mature and accomplished, starting shyly and then turning bold and confident, as she belts out 'It Don't Worry Me'. In some ways, this final performance is just a twist ending, like the surprise assassination. The scene is easily misunderstood as evidence of Altman's cynicism and misanthropy. He's just killed off the character who is most adored within the world of the film, and the crowd, instead of panicking or weeping, is lulled into submission by a song that seems to expressly declare that things are going terribly, but there's no reason to care. Has Sueleen lost the capacity to care, seemingly catatonic and forgotten on the side of the stage? Is this

not just Nashville but also America, after JFK, RFK, MLK, Chicago 1968, Watts and Detroit? Or more specifically, in the context of the 1970s, after Vietnam, Watergate, Kent State, Attica, impeachment and recession? If Albuquerque is just telling the audience not to worry, then yes, apathy is all that Americans have left. But of course that's not what she is doing. She's using a public performance – her public voice finally audible, her victory over her husband finally accomplished – to rally people emotionally to go on against all odds.

Here, suddenly, *Nashville* is a musical, or at least *like* a musical, a genre in which music can be transformative and pull people together, if not politically or for the long term, at least fleetingly, via feelings. It might seem like a strange way to end the film, and yet it's common to close out conventional musicals with a big uplifting number. The facile reading of the finale of *Nashville* is that 'It Don't Worry Me' is ironic and condescending, and that crowd members are too simple to understand that the words are not in their best interests. If this were true, Triplette's seduction of Bill and Mary applies to everyone: the crowd at the Parthenon are not politically astute, and they have been sold a bill of goods.

Yet, the song has already been used repeatedly in the film, and the words didn't matter much then. The first time was at the end of the traffic pile-up scene, when the chorus plays as Tricycle Man

rides away – it's actually the Black choir singing the song, much as they do at the end of the movie, but without Albuquerque's voice. Here, the music is little more than a punctuation mark to indicate the end of the scene. The second time is Tom singing the recorded song on a reel-to-reel player in the motel, as he contemptuously jostles Opal to throw her out of bed. What's important at this moment is not the song lyrics but the vanity of the whole scenario. The third time takes place at the Exit/In, when the crowd sings the song without music as a prompt to get the Bill, Mary and Tom trio to sing. It's one of their hits, and the crowd sings to celebrate it as such, not to convey that they feel unworried. In light of these previous iterations of 'It Don't Worry Me', the literalism of the lyrics may not be relevant in the concluding moments of the film. (It's worth adding, too, that Carradine wrote the song for *Emperor of the North*, a brutal 1973 film about hobos riding the rails during the Depression. Director Robert Aldrich ended up not using it, perhaps because lyrics like 'my spirit's high as it can be' were plainly at odds – on purpose, one presumes – with every aspect of the film.)

If we understand the *Nashville* crowd's singing as collective experience rather than as a declaration of apathy, the finale takes on a more nuanced and indeterminate meaning. By point of contrast, compare this ending to the finale of *All That Jazz* (1979), a dark film that adheres to musical conventions, merely reversing their affective intention and eliciting dystopian rather than utopian feelings. The picture ends with a zippy show tune about death and then, as the titles roll, an alarming, pounding, iconic Ethel Merman rendition of 'There's No Business Like Show Business' erupts. Director Bob Fosse's ironic, literal deployment of exactly those lyrics matters. It's quite the opposite of the ambiguous closing of *Nashville* with a song that may have little to do with how its singers feel.

Consider also Albuquerque's improvised spoken words that she inserts into her performance: 'Now, if we don't live peaceful, there's gonna be nothin' left in our graves except Clorox bottles and plastic fly swatters with red dots on 'em.' We are all going to die.

The question is: was it all for nought? To end up with more than Clorox bottles and mass-produced fly swatters (which have 'something to do with the Industrial Revolution') is to reject domestic imprisonment – it is trapped housewives who run the white loads and scrub the bathroom tiles and kill the flies. It is also to reject the banal. Where, then, might the *sublime* lie, if only fleetingly? In the pathos-filled, potentially joyful release of the human voice.

The film is over. The camera tilts up, past a gigantic American flag, to a sky full of clouds. It looks like rain. What a beautiful day to be alive.

Coda: 'Exercise Your Right to Vote!'

Some fifty years after *Nashville*, it's hard to satirise American politics because things are simply too strange and terrifying on their own. As twenty-first century comedians and editorial cartoonists face the challenge of finding adequate words and images to mock the real-life black comedy and tragedy of Trump-era authoritarianism, *Nashville*'s kooky lines about oranges and Christmas and the flaws of the national anthem might seem almost quaint to a contemporary viewer. For some, *Nashville*, with its anti-Nixon undercurrent, may even provoke nostalgia for an earlier era of political villains capable of at least pretending to respect civic and democratic norms.

To his credit, Altman never gave up on the power of political satire, although satire was not his only mode. In the interim between *Nashville* and his passing in 2006, the director remained committed to politically engaged work. *Secret Honor* (1984), for example, is a manic Nixon takedown. In *Nashville* Nixon was a pervasive undertow, but in *Secret Honor* he is the entire raging ocean. Ultimately, the production that perhaps most interestingly functions as a *Nashville* postscript is the eleven-episode HBO production *Tanner '88* (1988), a pointed attack on Reaganism. Here again Michael Murphy is cast in a political role, this time as a candidate for the presidency himself. Tanner's whole objective is to undo the right-wing damage of the Reagan years. At one point, he earnestly makes the argument for himself on TV, and on top of the set sit a Nixon–Agnew bumper sticker and a grotesque, clown-like miniature Reagan bust. Reagan appears again in the last episode as a ridiculous inflatable doll.

Tanner '88 never achieves the emotional or artistic intensity of *Nashville* but that's not what it's going for. Instead, using a mix of

Tanner '88 (1988)

scripted, improvised and documentary material, Altman tried to show
both the serious and amusing sides of what a political campaign
looked like as it was unfolding, material that was always just beyond
the borders of *Nashville*. The production does, however, visit the city
of Nashville in one episode. There, Tanner is the target of a weak
assassination attempt, following which he has a sit-down with the
famous country singer Waylon Jennings, who supports his campaign.
Tanner then goes to meet an old friend who works at Fisk University,
the local historically Black institution and home of the choir that
performed in *Nashville*. He walks in on his friend during Fisk choir
practice and pulls him aside to chat, hoping for an endorsement. It's
a blow out because someone in his campaign alerts the media to the
meeting, and the friend feels betrayed. This is an unfortunate turn of
events, but it's more sad than dark. *Tanner '88* satirises the role of the
media in promoting or harming politicians, but it's ultimately not a
cynical production.

In the end, Tanner fails to win the Democratic nomination
because he leans too far left, and any supporters leaning in that

direction would rather go for Jesse Jackson, anyway. Tanner began his campaign as a liberal advocating drug legalisation, yet he was moved by his conversations with Black voters in Detroit and seemed taken with their argument that the only way to stop the drug problem was to crack down on the countries producing and exporting the drugs. It's a jab at Reagan's Iran–Contra scandal, and indicates an approach to policy clearly more radical than the policies of the Democratic front runner, Michael Dukakis. Further reinforcing that Tanner is too liberal (or just too eccentric) to win, his proposed cabinet includes Ralph Nader as Attorney General, Gloria Steinem as Secretary of Health and Human Services, Art Buchwald as Ambassador to France and Studs Terkel as Secretary of Labor.

What really stands out in *Tanner '88*, when viewed in contrast to *Nashville*, is that it digs deep into the crevices of how politics work, how politicians' images are constructed, how voters are wooed in the New Hampshire primary and elsewhere, and how journalists desperately seek stories. At one point, Altman even shows Tanner's control room during the Democratic convention, when his team attempts and fails to spur an open convention, in which delegates could vote for Tanner instead of Dukakis. Of course, it can't work, as Dukakis is the insider choice, and it turns out Jackson's team was playing Tanner's all along. There's a hard observational edge to the whole show, and this is amplified by the use of videotape that signified cheap and therefore 'authentic' documentary at the time, though it is muddy and aesthetically off-putting to the contemporary eye.

One of the challenges of the production was that every viewer knew the ending: it may have included cameos by real political operatives like Pat Robertson, but Tanner was a fictional character who was not going to be nominated on the Democratic ticket in 1988. So the excitement of the show came not in the destination but the journey, which resonates with the whole corpus of Altman's work. *Tanner '88* was co-written by the director and *Doonesbury* cartoonist Garry Trudeau, but of course improvised as it moved along, with episodes released as they were produced, sometimes within days of having been shot, and all of it responding to the real ups and downs of the presidential election cycle. In his trademark style, as in *The Long Goodbye*, Altman wove variations of a single song throughout the production, a patriotic ditty entitled 'Exercise Your Right to Vote', which could be hummed, used as a stand-in for Happy Birthday or even performed, rather ridiculously, by a hair metal band at a fundraiser.

Altman loved the whole thing; as Murphy told me, he was

totally 'in the moment' and having the time of his life doing that series. He was totally focused ... more so than I'd ever seen him ...'cause we were doing it in real time and reacting to events that were happening in the news on a daily basis. He was even able to occasionally bag network footage before it went on the air and cut it into the show. It was really quite an experience ... a real Altman adventure. He had a cynical love for politics and the country in general ... loved exposing and commenting on the stuff that goes on ... and *Tanner* was kind of a step beyond *Nashville* for him in that he got to mess with the real politicians in stressful situations and, again, in real time.

Altman himself said that in *Nashville* Murphy 'had played the dark side of Tanner'.[46] Tanner was a better man than Triplette, and probably Hal Phillip Walker, too, but he still lost.

Viewed fifty years later, *Nashville* is still funny and sad. It also strikes one as simultaneously cynical and intensely earnest about the microscopic webs of human interaction and macroscopic webs of American politics. If it was dubious and also funny to claim in 1975 that Americans 'must be doing something right to last two hundred years', we have no reason to feel more certain of rightness as we hit the 250-year mark. Altman remained in the desert of cynicism up until the end, but he kept hoping for rain. As Americans face the looming, violent forces of authoritarianism, fascism, white nationalism and misogyny, it remains harder than ever to keep hoping for rain. Life may be a one-way street, but we can still tilt our gaze upward, towards the clouds. Hope lies less in what we see than in the act of looking.

Notes

1 Geoff Andrew, 'The Sprawling Brilliance of Robert Altman's *Nashville*', *Sight and Sound* vol. 31 no. 5 (June 2021). Available at: <https://www.bfi.org. uk/sight-and-sound/features/robert- altman-nashville-1975-sprawling- american-masterpiece> (accessed 9 September 2024).

2 Jan Stuart, *The Nashville Chronicles: The Making of Robert Altman's Masterpiece* (New York: Limelight Editions, 2004), p. 205.

3 Chuck Sack and Joan Tewkesbury, 'Joan Tewkesbury on Screenwriting: An Interview', *Film/Literature Quarterly* vol. 6 no. 1 (Winter 1978), p. 11.

4 Molly Haskell, *From Reverence to Rape: The Treatment of Women in the Movies*, 2nd edn (Chicago: University of Chicago Press, 1987). After offering a stellar list of strong female performances, Haskell soberly lists the sorts of roles that the women played: 'whores, quasi- whores, jilted mistresses, emotional cripples … sex-starved spinsters, psychotics … and ballbreakers. That's what little girls of the sixties and seventies are made of' (pp. 327–8). Haskell singles out Altman's *3 Women* and Fellini's *City of Women* (1980) as 'the only works of art by men to take seriously, and with courageously admitted anxiety, the possibility of women abandoning men and forming a society of their own' (p. 394).

5 See 'Last Picture Show Love Triangle: Polly Platt, The Invisible Woman Part 3', in *You Must Remember This: Polly Platt: The Invisible Woman Archive* (podcast), 8 June 2020. Available at: <http://www. youmustrememberthispodcast.com/

episodes/2020/6/1/last-picture-show- love-triangle-polly-platt-the-invisible- woman-part-3> (accessed 10 December 2024). A sources list for all ten episodes is available here: <http://www. youmustrememberthispodcast.com/ episodes/2020/5/26/polly-platt-season- sources>.

6 Justin Wyatt, 'Economic Constraints/ Economic Opportunities: Robert Altman as Auteur', *The Velvet Light Trap* vol. 38 (Autumn 1996), pp. 51–67.

7 Connie Byrne and William O. Lopez, 'Nashville', *Film Quarterly* vol. 29 no. 2 (Winter 1975–6), p. 14.

8 Pauline Kael, 'Robert Altman's Funny, Epic Vision of America', *New Yorker*, 23 February 1975.

9 Paul Gardner, 'Altman Surveys "Nashville" and Sees "Instant" America', *New York Times*, 13 June 1975.

10 Tom Wicker, '"Nashville" – Dark Perceptions in a Country-Music Comedy: A Cascade of Greed, Cruelty, Hysteria', *New York Times*, 15 June 1975.

11 Dan Blim, '"You Don't Belong in Nashville!": Politics, Country Music, and the Reception of Robert Altman's *Nashville*', *Music & Politics* vol. 16 no. 2 (Summer 2022), pp. 11–12. See also Blim on how Nashville's country music stars responded to the film, on the film's under-performance at the box office, and on country music and conservative politics.

12 Stephen L. Betts, 'Flashback: Robert Altman's "Nashville" Angers Country Stars', *Rolling Stone*, 11 June 2015.

13 Letter to the Editor from Thomas H. Jackson, '"Nashville" Promotes City', *The Tennessean*, 1 November 1975, p. 6.

14 Eugene Wyatt, 'Altman Goal: Crush Stereotype of South', *The Tennessean*, 6 June 1975, p. 57.

15 <https://www.presidency.ucsb. edu/documents/remarks-the-grand-ole-opry-house-nashville-tennessee> (accessed 1 December 2024).

16 'Turned off by rock's revolutionary sentiment, anti-war messaging, and sexual and drug-inspired hedonism, country fans embraced the music's appeal to stability, tradition and patriotism.' Blim, '"You Don't Belong in Nashville!"', p. 3.

17 Tom Wicker cited in George F. Will, 'A Metaphor for America?', *Washington Post*, 30 June 1975.

18 Will, 'A Metaphor for America?'.

19 Sack and Tewkesbury, 'Joan Tewkesbury on Screenwriting', p. 20.

20 Patrick Buchanan, '"Nashville" is Slander on Celluloid', *Chicago Tribune*, 29 July 1975.

21 On Buchanan see Nicole Hemmer, *Partisans: The Conservative Revolutionaries Who Remade American Politics in the 1990s* (New York: Basic Books, 2022).

22 There are multiple sources on Buchanan's advice to burn the tapes. The man himself briefly recounts the story here: 'Burn It', C-SPAN, 24 May 2017. Available at: <https://www.c-span. org/video/?c4782436/user-clip-burn-it> (accessed 18 January 2025).

23 Mark Minett, 'Sponsoring the Hollywood Renaissance: Reappraising Altman's Industrial Films', in Adrian Danks (ed.), *A Companion to Robert Altman* (Chichester: Wiley-Blackwell, 2015), pp. 21–43.

24 Ibid., p. 34.

25 'Dorian Leigh, Unconventional American Model and the Face of the 1940s and 50s', *Guardian*, 11 July 2008.

26 David Thompson (ed.), *Altman on Altman* (New York: Farrar, Straus and Giroux, 2006), pp. 39–40.

27 Sack and Tewkesbury, 'Joan Tewkesbury on Screenwriting', p. 15.

28 Nick Dawson, '"That's the Movie, That's the Kind of Overlapping Mess That Bob Loves": Joan Tewkesbury on Writing Nashville', *Filmmaker,* 6 December 2013. Available at: <https:// filmmakermagazine.com/82780-thats-the-movie-thats-the-kind-of-overlapping-mess-that-bob-loves-joan-tewkesbury-on-writing-nashville/> (accessed 1 September 2024).

29 Sack and Tewkesbury, 'Joan Tewkesbury on Screenwriting', p. 11.

30 David Greenberg, *Nixon's Shadow: The History of an Image* (New York: W. W. Norton, 2003); Joe McGinniss, *The Selling of the President 1968* (New York: Trident, 1969).

31 Thompson (ed.), *Altman on Altman*, p. 17.

32 Altman discusses his feelings on audience viewing habits, as well as his interest in a wide range of film-makers and films, in Thompson (ed.), *Altman on Altman*.

33 Virginia Wright Wexman, '*Nashville*: Second City Performance Comes to Hollywood', in Danks (ed.), *A Companion to Robert Altman*, p. 377. Another idea was to release two versions of the film theatrically, *Nashville Red* and *Nashville Blue*, to be screened theatrically on alternating nights. Some versions of the story have

Red and *Blue*, two hours each, shown on TV.

34 Stuart, *The Nashville Chronicles*, p. 121.

35 Sack and Tewkesbury, 'Joan Tewkesbury on Screenwriting', p. 14.

36 Vincent Canby, 'A Satire, a Melodrama, a Celebration', *New York Times*, 15 June 1975; Kael, 'Robert Altman's Funny, Epic Vision'.

37 'Robert Altman and Gary Trudeau on Tanner '88', Criterion Channel video, 2004.

38 At his peak, Gould was in high demand and may have even kneecapped himself with overexposure. 'He appeared in eleven films between 1968 and 1973 at a time when comparable figures such as Dustin Hoffman and Barbra Streisand … averaged less than one a year.' David Cook, *Lost Illusions: American Cinema in the Shadow of Watergate and Vietnam, 1970–1979* (Berkeley: University of California Press, 2002), p. 340.

39 Sack and Tewkesbury, 'Joan Tewkesbury on Screenwriting', p. 17.

40 Stuart, *The Nashville Chronicles*, p. 252.

41 Dawson, '"That's the Movie"'.

42 Aniko Bodroghkozy, *Equal Time: Television and the Civil Rights Movement* (Urbana: University of Illinois Press, 2012), pp. 85–7.

43 Materials on the original screenplay and shooting script are available in the Altman archival collection at the University of Michigan. Available at: <https://findingaids.lib.umich.edu/catalog/umich-scl-altman3_al_21cc74fa6e2d9267e90569b1de07ce17d18d1d03#contents> (accessed 18 January 2025). A version of the script that resonates strongly with but is not identical to the release version of the film was also published: Joan Tewkesbury, *Nashville* (New York: Bantam, 1976).

44 Heather Hendershot, *When the News Broke: Chicago 1968 and the Polarizing of America* (Chicago, IL: University of Chicago Press, 2022).

45 Stuart, *The Nashville Chronicles*, pp. 129–30.

46 Thompson (ed.), *Altman on Altman*, p. 144.

Credits

Nashville
USA
1975

Director
Robert Altman
Production Company
American Broadcasting
Company
Paramount Pictures
Corporation

ABC Entertainment
presents
A Jerry Weintraub
production
A Robert Altman film
© 1975 American
Broadcasting Companies,
Inc.

Executive Producers
Martin Starger
Jerry Weintraub
Producer
Robert Altman
Associate Producers
Robert Eggenweiler
Scott Bushnell
Production Co-ordinator
Kelly Marshall
**Assistant to the
Producer**
Jac Cashin
Production Assistants
Angel Dominguez
Ron Hecht
Steve Altman
Mark Eggenweiler
Maysie Hoy

Allan Highfill
Roger Frappier
Production Secretary
Elaine Bradish
Assistant Directors
Tommy Thompson
Alan Rudolph
Script Supervisor
Joyce King
Screenplay
Joan Tewkesbury
Director of Photography
Paul Lohmann
Camera Operator
Ed Koons
Electrical Gaffers
Randy Glass
Mike Marlett
Grips
Harry Rez
Eddie Lara
Editors
Sidney Levin
Dennis Hill
Assistant Editors
Tony Lombardo
Tom Walls
Property Master
Bob Anderson
Wardrobe
Jules Melillo
Make-up
Tommy Thompson
Hairstylist
Ann Wadlington
Title Design
Dan Perri
**Music Arranged and
Supervised by**
Richard Baskin

Music Recordists
Gene Eichelberger
Johnny Rosen
Sound
Jim Webb
Chris McLaughlin
Re-recording Mixer
Richard Portman
Sound Editor
William A. Sawyer
Assistant Sound Editor
Randy Kelley
Political Campaign
Thomas Hal Phillips
Soundtrack
'200 Years', lyrics by
Henry Gibson, music by
Richard Baskin; 'Yes, I
Do', lyrics and music by
Richard Baskin and Lily
Tomlin; 'Down to the
River', lyrics and music
by Ronee Blakley; 'Let
Me Be the One', lyrics
and music by Richard
Baskin; 'Sing a Song',
lyrics and music by Joe
Raposo; 'The Heart of a
Gentle Woman', lyrics
and music by Dave Peel;
'Bluebird', lyrics and
music by Ronee Blakley;
'The Day I Looked Jesus
in the Eye', lyrics and
music by Richard Baskin
and Robert Altman;
'Memphis', lyrics and
music by Karen Black;
'I Don't Know if I Found
it in You', lyrics and

music by Karen Black; 'For the Sake of the Children', lyrics and music by Richard Baskin and Richard Reicheg; 'Keep a' Goin'', lyrics by Henry Gibson, music by Richard Baskin and Henry Gibson; 'Swing Low, Sweet Chariot', arrangements by Millie Clements; 'Rolling Stone', lyrics and music by Karen Black; 'Honey', lyrics and music by Keith Carradine; 'Tapedeck in his Tractor', lyrics and music by Ronee Blakley; 'Dues', lyrics and music by Ronee Blakley; 'I Never Get Enough', lyrics and music by Richard Baskin and Ben Raleigh; 'Rose's Café', lyrics and music by Allan Nicholls; 'Old Man Mississippi', lyrics and music by Juan Grizzle; 'My Baby's Cookin' in Another Man's Pan', lyrics and music by Jonnie Barnett; 'One, I Love You', lyrics and music by Richard Baskin; 'I'm Easy', lyrics and music by Keith Carradine; 'It Don't Worry Me', lyrics and music by Keith Carradine; 'Since You've Gone', lyrics and music by Gary Busey; 'Trouble in the U.S.A.', lyrics and music by Arlene Barnett, performed by Avis Barnett and the Barnetts; 'My Idaho Home', lyrics and music by Ronee Blakley

CAST
David Arkin
Norman
Barbara Baxley
Lady Pearl
Ned Beatty
Delbert Reese
Karen Black
Connie White
Ronee Blakley
Barbara Jean
Timothy Brown
Tommy Brown
Keith Carradine
Tom Frank
Geraldine Chaplin
Opal
Robert Doqui
Wade
Shelley Duvall
L. A. Joan/Martha
Allen Garfield
Barnett
Henry Gibson
Haven Hamilton
Scott Glenn
PFC Glenn Kelly
Jeff Goldblum
Tricycle Man

Barbara Harris
Albuquerque
David Hayward
Kenny Fraiser
Michael Murphy
John Triplette
Allan Nicholls
Bill
Dave Peel
Bud Hamilton
Cristina Raines
Mary
Bert Remsen
Star
Lily Tomlin
Linnea Reese
Gwen Welles
Sueleen Gay
Keenan Wynn
Mr Green
James Dan Calvert
Jimmy Reese
Donna Denton
Donna Reese
Merle Kilgore
Trout
Carol McGinnis
Jewel
Sheila Bailey
Patti Bryant
Smokey Mountain Laurel
Richard Baskin
Frog, piano player
Jonnie Barnett
himself
Vassar Clements
himself
Misty Mountain Boys
themselves

Sue Barton
herself
Elliott Gould
himself
Julie Christie
herself

Production Details
35mm
2.35:1
Colour
MPAA no.: 24225
Running time:
160 minutes

Release Details
US theatrical release
on 2 July 1975 by
Paramount Pictures
UK theatrical release
on 18 September 1975
by Cinema International
Corporation